POP GOES THE GOSPEL

POP GOES THE *GOSPEL*

Rock in the church

John Blanchard

with Peter Anderson & Derek Cleave

 EVANGELICAL PRESS

EVANGELICAL PRESS
12 Wooler Street, Darlington, Co Durham, DL1 1RQ,
England

© Evangelical Press
First published 1983
Enlarged and revised edition 1989
Second impression 1991

British Library Cataloguing Publication Data available

ISBN 0 85234 263 2

Cover picture by courtesy of A. Jay Photography

Typeset in Great Britain by Outset Graphics, Hartlepool
Printed in Great Britain by Cox & Wyman, Reading

Contents

Preface

The use of pop music in evangelism has become a very 'hot potato' in recent years. Everybody has an opinion on the subject. Pop gospel turns some people on; it switches others off. Some see it as a blessing from heaven, others as a curse from hell. Thousands of Christians (mainly young) would travel almost any distance to get to a gospel concert – and would be met by hordes of fellow-Christians (mainly older) trying to get away from it!

There seems no neutrality on the issue. Right across theological and denominational boundaries – to say nothing of age ranges – people are getting very hot under the collar as they argue their particular line. Often the arguments generate more heat than light. Sometimes opponents seem unable to make the important distinction between people and principles, or the equally important one between fact and fiction.

The time has come to take a calm, balanced, thorough and biblical look at the whole subject of what we might call 'entertainment evangelism': *this book is an attempt to do so*. We do not write as experts in any field of music, but we do have access to what the experts have to say and can therefore quote them freely. Much more importantly, we have access to the Bible, 'the living and enduring word of God' (1 Peter 1:23), and we have tried

to bring its commands, warnings, examples and principles to bear on the subject at every stage.

Pop gospel is one of the most important issues facing
evangelism in large areas of the world today and as we
have got to grips with the subject it has been exhilarating
to see how relevant the Bible is to every part of it.
Perhaps our greatest rediscovery has been that the Bible
is 'the law that gives *freedom*' (James 2:12). To natural
ears, that sounds like a contradiction in terms. Law and
liberty seem like opposites – but in Christian language
they are not. For instance, submission to Scripture sets
us free from being tied to *trends,* which swirl around us
in all art forms, but particularly in music, where the
changes can be so sudden and severe. On the other
hand, it also sets us free from *tradition,* which can cramp
us into one particular culture or style. It sets us free from
peer group pressure, the insistence of the majority,
which can rob us of the privilege of genuinely free
choice. It sets us free from relying on our *emotions,*
which are such notoriously unreliable guides. Above all,
it sets us free from the subtle tyranny of *self,* the second
worst enemy we have.

We are making no great claims for what we have written, but it is our prayer that this little book will help
many Christians to set aside their prejudices and preferences, think the whole issue through *biblically* and then
act with 'the obedience that comes from faith' (Romans
1:5).

We would like to thank Andrew Anderson, Brian
Edwards and Tony Seagar, who read the early draft of
the first edition and made many helpful suggestions. We
are also grateful to Mrs Joy Hills for her excellent typing
of the finished manuscript, and to Richard Frost for permission to use his unpublished poem on page 143.

In this second edition we have updated many of the

quotations used to illustrate our arguments, considerably reinforced certain sections, taken a closer look at the Christian music scene and included additional material on subjects such as backward masking.

We have also added an appendix on the neurophysiology of rock music, and wish to thank Drs Daniel and Bernadette Skubik of the Department of Philosophy at the Research School of Science at the Adelaide National University in Australia for their kind permission to include this abbreviation of some of the results of their detailed research in this area.

1.
A slice of history

We live in a world that is massaged by music. It seems to be everywhere. Background music fills the air in super-markets, department stores, warehouses, factories, car showrooms, restaurants and countless other public places. Travel by ship, and it is there, from stem to stern; go by airplane, and it is there, too. Escape all of that, get home and settle down to watch television, and it is there again, whether the programme is *Neighbours* or *Newsnight, Eastenders* or *Everyman*. Decide to watch nothing except the news, and you are not allowed to see the headlines until you have heard the music. Spin the tuner on your radio and there are channels devoted almost entirely to music of one kind or another. Music's penetration into our modern society is nothing short of a phenomenon, something that has a profoundly significant impact on the lives of millions of people around the world.

If this is true of music in general, it is especially true of what is loosely called 'pop music' or 'rock music' – the terms are imprecise as we shall see later – which has such a massive impact on the lives of young people in particular.

In the beginning. . .?

In his fluent paperback *Summer in the City,* Malcolm

Doney says, 'Rock music is not simply another branch of popular culture. It has shown itself to be perhaps the most significant art form to emerge this century.'[1] What is more, he sees its importance as being far greater than musical; he calls it 'a gauge of the shifts in young people's attitudes towards sex, authority, taste, their contemporaries and ethics'.[2]

Another observer commented, 'As truly as the nineteenth century had belonged to authors and philosophers because of the printing press, so the twentieth century belongs to the musician because of records and radio.'[3] An American music magazine advertised, 'If you are a corporate executive trying to understand what is happening to youth today, you cannot afford to be without *Rolling Stone*. If you are a student, a professor, a parent, this is your life because you already know that rock and roll is more than just music; it is the energy centre of the new culture and your revolution.'[4]

If these statements are even half true, rock music is something of great significance that has 'happened' during the lifetime of everyone in the world born before 1950. But did it just 'happen'? We will never begin to understand rock music until we discover something of its beginnings, but as with so many things, that is easier said than done.

Having said that, some people find it no problem whatever: all rock music stems directly from the devil, and its journey can be traced very simply – from hell to the African jungle, from the African jungle to America, and then, on twentieth-century airwaves, from America to the rest of the world. QED! But that is neither factual nor fair. Blanket condemnation of the whole of today's pop scene by condensing its history into one searing sentence certainly abbreviates discussion, but it hardly helps to arrive at the truth.

The fact is that rock draws from many streams and is

very complex. It is a Mississippi of music, with many different tributaries flowing into the vast river of sound we are now hearing, and it is virtually impossible to trace all of those tributaries back to their sources.

Roots

Even if we do not buy the 'All rock is African jungle music' line, there can be no serious doubt that the roots of rock do run back into the West African slave culture of the fifteenth century, which was eventually taken to the West Indies and the southern part of what is now the United States. Primitive, home-made instruments were later replaced by the clarinet, trumpet, cornet and trombone, with the piano, guitar, banjo, double-bass and drums eventually forming the 'rhythm section'.

Music played a very important role in the lives of the slaves, enabling them to express their emotions in terms of their own traditional culture rather than in those dictated by their grim conditions. Yet eventually they began to assimilate some of the other musical values with which they were surrounded – ballads from Elizabethan England, quadrilles from France, traditional Spanish dances, (which were particularly popular in Louisiana) and, of course, the country music that was already becoming 'American' in its own right.

In the development of all art forms, there is a mixture of assimilation and innovation and the same was true in the development of popular music. Slowly, distinctive styles began to emerge and to spread and this continued right through the time of the slaves' emancipation in 1865 and on into the twentieth century itself. Blues (slow and sad), rhythm and blues (more heavily accented), gospel (adaptation of hymn tunes), rag-time (strongly syncopated) and jazz (lots of improvisation) – one trend led to another. Nothing was entirely new; every development of style borrowed something from the past and reflected something of the present, mirroring its moods and expressing them in popular form. Steve Lawhead summarizes it by saying that these developing musical styles 'were formed in the give-and-take of many cultural backgrounds (German, Czech, French, Irish, English and others) over many years,'[5] and adds, 'Even the music of Africa did not originate spontaneously on its own. It was shaped by its contact with Europe, Asia and the Middle East.'[6]

Not that dispersing the roots of rock sanctifies it. The original blues singers rejected the Christian faith as part of a hostile white culture, and placed a heavy emphasis on 'the pleasure of this world, particularly the enjoyment of illicit sex . . . Heaven, if it existed, was to be peopled with dancing girls.'[7] Rod Gruver says that the blues poets insisted that 'No other love can compare with the love that comes either before or outside marriage.'[8]

These examples alone serve to remind us of one simple fact – that in *all* cultures we must expect to find an underlying trend of values that are not just sub-Christian but anti-Christian. Man is *fallen,* and his fallenness comes to the surface in every age, in every country and in every part of his culture. It is all part of what the Bible means when it says, 'All have sinned and *fall short* of the glory of God' (Romans 3:23) and our italics emphasize the fact that man's fallenness is a continuing reality.

Haley's Comets

Popular music after the end of World War II was a tired hangover from what went before – romantic, sentimental and *predictable.* But by the early nineteen-fifties the new generation of American teenager was discovering other sounds – updated versions of blues and rhythm and blues, in which 'the vocals were rough and uncompromising, the lyrics personal and explicit'.[9] Primarily, it was black music, but soon white groups began to play it. Leading the way was a middle-aged country and western group called Bill Haley and the Comets. They would hardly have been typecast as revolutionaries, but by the time they had recorded 'Shake, rattle and roll' (toning down the words), 'Crazy, man, crazy' (the first white rock 'n' roll record to hit the charts) and 'Rock around the Clock' (which eventually sold fifteen million as a single) popular music had been catapulted into a new era.

Elvis

What was now needed was the man to match the music, someone young, raw, mean and exciting – and along came the very man, a one-time choirboy called Elvis Presley. Presley was worshipped by some and hated by others. To his millions of fans he was 'the King'; to others he was not far short of the personification of everything evil. He appeared arrogant, sensuous, obscene. He was said to consult with a psychic in Colorado, and to be heavily into drugs. One of his bodyguards claimed that the rock 'n' roll idol's buttocks were 'so punctured with needle marks that there was hardly room left for an injection'.[10] When he died in 1977 at the age of forty-two, 'Elvis the Pelvis' had earned 4.3 billion dollars from a career which remains without parallel in the history of popular music.

The lads from Liverpool

Elvis opened the floodgates for hundreds of imitators and followers in the same, raw, aggressive, sensual style, yet, surprisingly, the vogue did not last very long. By the end of the nineteen-fifties rock 'n' roll was no longer dominant, its place on centre stage taken by something much more generally acceptable – folk music. Folk was almost 'thinking man's music' compared to rock 'n' roll. It spoke about serious political issues (it was the perfect vehicle for the protest songs of people like Joan Baez and the legendary Bob Dylan). What is more, it was *quieter,* with the acoustic guitar taking the place of the electric version with its stacks of speakers to amplify the sound.

But that all changed in 1963 with the arrival of the Beatles. However tame their music may now sound to many people, the Fabulous Four hit the music scene like a runaway bulldozer. Their sound has been described as 'fresh, new and inventive'[11] – but to others it was outrageous, irreverent and dangerous. What *is* certain is that it was sensationally popular, leading John Lennon to make his now legendary statement that the Beatles were more popular than Jesus Christ. As Malcolm Doney comments, 'The Beatles became more than hugely famous, they became *cosmic.*'[12]

The Beatles' brand of music was generally less abrasive and raw-edged than was usually the case with rock 'n' roll and they were the major influence in the need to coin a new phrase that would embrace the widening range of Beatles-inspired sound. 'Rock' became the post-Beatle word for all kinds of contemporary popular music – and serves the same purpose today, even though that can be misleading at times.

The Stones and other stars

The late sixties saw the rise of the hippie movement, with the Beatles' Sergeant Pepper's Lonely Hearts Club Band becoming 'the anthem of the hip culture'.[13] Then came the gigantic outdoor festivals. Daddy of them all was Woodstock (New York) which was attended by 500,000 rock fans in August 1969 and has been described as 'three days of dope, sex and music'.[14]

Soon afterwards came Altamont, near San Francisco, when the hippie dream turned to ashes. Three fans died of drugs, and one was stabbed and beaten to death in front of stage while the band played on. The band playing on was The Rolling Stones.

The Stones' image was clear, but hardly clean. Nik Cohn says, 'They were mean and nasty ... and they beat out the toughest, crudest, most offensive noise any English band had ever made.'[15] Derek Jewell agrees: 'They projected the harshest, nastiest, sweaty-sexiest and most pointedly offensive musical image yet to frighten all law-abiding Britons with daughters under twenty-one out of their minds.'[16] Drugs, promiscuity and occultism have all been part of the Stones' package – and their influence has been enormous. Malcolm Doney claims, 'It is difficult to exaggerate the impact of The Rolling Stones. They brought upon themselves more scorn and adult hysteria than any musicians before or since.'[17]

Others who shared their heyday included performers such as The Who, Led Zeppelin and Alice Cooper. Following them we had punk rock, with the music described by Derek Jewell as 'the latest musical garbage bred by our troubled culture'[18], and the punk rockers as those who loved 'hate, aggression, apathy, lust, alcohol, anarchy'.[19] Yet punk rock never really made it and soon the rock world moved on to the next change . . . and the one after that . . . Yesterday's stars are fading, tomorrow's rising in the sky – and the appetites of those who listen are apparently insatiable. In David Wilkerson's words, rock music is 'the biggest mass addiction in the world's history'.[20] Whatever one's personal opinions on the phenomenon, it seems difficult to disagree with Steve Lawhead when he writes, 'For so long as young people feel repressed and awkward, as long as society can indulge one affluent and self-centred generation after another, as long as there is electricity, there will be rock music.'[21]

2.
Identity crisis

Before trying to link rock music's past with its present use in Christian circles, we ought to ask two specific questions. Firstly, what is rock music? Secondly, what is Christian music? The answer to the first question is about as straightforward as the answer to the question, 'How long is a piece of string?'; the answer to the second is rather more difficult!

To begin at the beginning, what do we mean when we use the phrase 'rock music'? After all, there is sweet rock and acid rock, soft rock and hard rock, glam rock and glitter rock, folk rock and punk rock – 'everything from gay rock to God rock'[1] – to say nothing of reggae, heavy metal, new wave, disco, new romantic and jazz funk. No wonder Derek Jewell can write, 'No one has satisfactorily *defined* rock . . . you suggest its properties rather than pin it down firmly.'[2] These days 'rock' is a label which loosely covers the whole range of contemporary popular music. Yet there are certain characteristics basic to what we could almost call 'traditional' rock music. What are they, and how do they relate to the use of rock as an evangelistic vehicle?

On and on and on and on . . .

One of the basic constituents of rock music is constant

repetition. Listen to any rock record you choose, and one of its major features will be the constant repetition of chord patterns, beat, a narrow range of notes or a rhythmic figure. Professor Frank Garlock, Chairman of the Music Theory Department at Bob Jones University, tells of spending an entire week listening to 1,000 rock records and discovering that only three had anything approaching a balanced structure. All the rest consisted of the constant repetition of chordal, melodic or rhythmic patterns.

There is obviously no 'law' about the amount of variety that is needed before a piece of music becomes 'legitimate'; the most we can say is that variety is one of the marks of any good music, regardless of style. Some people might say that there is considerable repetition in certain classical music, and this is true. But generally speaking (there are notable exceptions) it is *creative*, with subtle variations woven into it. Is there honestly any comparison between, say, the repetition in a Vivaldi concerto movement and that in Led Zeppelin's 'Whole Lotta Love' (widely considered a classic piece of rock)? Quite apart from the erotic elements and simulated orgasm, 'Whole Lotta Love' has about as much variety of sound as a pneumatic drill.

This insistent repetition immediately raises warning cones about the suitability of rock music in evangelism, because *constant repetition has a hypnotic effect*. Professor William Shafer, a non-Christian sociologist, says, 'What is undeniable about rock is its hypnotic power. It has gripped millions of young people around the world and transformed their lives.'[3] Dr Granville Knight agrees: 'There is no question in my mind about the hypnotic effect of these songs.' So does Dr W. J. Bryan: 'Children are being hypnotized without their knowledge, and that is the really insidious part about these records. The more often the hypnotism is repeated the higher the susceptibility of the subject.' In the course of his specialized study, Andrew Salter has indicated that rock music is an ideal vehicle for individual or mass hypnosis.[4] Many other experts in this area have said the same kind of thing. In his book *Are the kids all right?* John Fuller writes, 'Rock music in particular has been demonstrated to be both powerful and addictive, as well as capable of producing a subtle form of hypnosis in which the subject, though not completely under trance, is still in a highly suggestive state.'[5] Writing in *Journal of Christian Healing*, R. Mesmer says, 'Because drums intervene in the normal ongoing split-second alteration between the right and left hemisphere during usual states of consciousness, rock music can well be regarded as generating an altered state of consciousness.'[6] In *The Neurobiology of Ritual Dance* B. W. Lex says, 'An altered state of consciousness or trance state is initiated by many cultural practices which activate and place the right hemisphere in pre-eminence while at the same time inhibiting or holding constant the capacities of the left hemisphere,' and cites as examples 'responding to the rhythms of chanting, dancing, singing and percussion instruments'.[7] Even more telling is this statement by the late Jimi Hendrix, one of the most dynamic and influential superstars in rock music history: 'Atmospheres are going to come through music, because the music is a spiritual thing of its own. You can hypnotize people with the music and when you get them at their weakest point you can preach into the subconscious what you want to say.'[8]

This obviously has very serious implications for the use of rock music in evangelism. Any medium of presentation that induces any loss of self-control or awareness and makes the listener unusually susceptible to whatever suggestions are made by the lyrics is surely dangerous, and will almost certainly encourage a response that will be largely psychological instead of that which God requires, that we should worship him 'in spirit and in truth' (John 4:24).

Drummer's holiday

As with constant repetition, driving beat is an indispensable ingredient of rock. As Bob Larson puts it, 'Whatever harmonic or melodic or verbal sophistication rock may contain, it would never appeal as it does without the undergirding of its simple, repetitive, pounding beat.'[9] As with repetition, rhythm plays a valid part in all music, but in rock music rhythm is replaced by a relentless, driving beat. The difference between this beat and genuine rhythm has been well put by Igor Stravinsky: 'Rhythm doesn't really exist, because no rhythmic proportion or relaxation exists.'[10] Bob Larson says much the same thing: 'Unlike other forms of music which may reveal melodic inventiveness, the focus of rock is usually on the beat. It is a drummer's holiday . . . I have known drummers who have actually had self-induced orgasms after several hours of incessant drumming.'[11] Elsewhere, he acknowledges the effects of this: 'An incessantly driving pulsated beat pattern is not inherently evil, but when applied for a protracted period of time at a high volume level, its spiritual effect can be devastating, especially at live concerts. Like any repetitious assault on one's neurosensory apparatus, it may shut down the conscious mental processes. It is the same technique used in eastern meditative processes such as Transcendental Meditation.'[12]

Even without thinking in terms of such extremes, it must be obvious that excessive beat has real dangers. There is evidence, for instance, to suggest that when the beat overrides the other elements in a song the communication level is significantly changed to one which is primarily physical and often specifically sexual. Rock musician Tom McSloy has no doubts about this: 'To *get* into rock you have to *give* in to it, let it inside, flow with it to the point where it consumes you, and all you can feel or hear or think about is the music.'[13] That is an alarming statement, but it ties in perfectly with some words written by someone who comes at it from a completely different angle, the well-known British preacher, Dr Martyn Lloyd-Jones. In his classic book *Preaching and Preachers* he has a section in which he warns of the dangers of preachers making a direct attack on either the emotions or the will. In it he writes, 'We can become drunk on music – there is no question about that. Music can have the effect of creating an emotional state in which the mind is no longer functioning as it should be, and no longer discriminating. I have known people to sing themselves into a state of intoxication without realizing what they were doing.'[14] We can take it for granted that he was not writing about a rock concert – so the point we are making is not part of an 'anti-rock' diatribe. What we are saying is that the element of relentless beat in rock music increases the danger of a shallow, emotional, unthinking response, made at the wrong level and for the wrong reasons. David Winter openly admits in his book *New Singer, New Song* that 'An incessant beat does erode a sense of responsibility in much the same way as alcohol does . . . You feel in the grip of a relentless stream of sound to which something very basic and primitive in the human nature responds.'[15] Surely this is a highly dangerous thing? To quote Lloyd-Jones again, 'The important point is that we should realize that *the effect produced in such a case is not produced by the truth . . .*'[16]

Dangerous decibels

As with repetition and beat, no time need be wasted in
proving that volume is an important element in rock
music, with huge stacks of equipment needed to produce
the required amount of amplification. This report by
Derek Jewell of a sell-out Albert Hall concert by the
British group The Cream (now disbanded but which
broke Beatles' attendance records in the United States)
tells us the kind of impact that can be made: 'It contained
some highly skilled, if perverse, talent – especially the
guitarist Eric Clapton. But its Albert Hall show was mis-
conceived, an attempt at a gigantic *tour de force,* with
the accent on force. I have never heard louder music. It
destroyed itself in sheer decibels. The juggernaut of
sound assaulted the stomach as well as being a danger to
the ear-drums. It was mind-fragmenting music, involving one in what the pop avant-garde fashionably calls
total experience. I don't want total experience in a concert hall . . . I want *musical* experiences . . .'[17]

Volume for volume's sake is one trademark of heavy
metal, which arrived in the late sixties with groups like
Deep Purple, Black Sabbath and Led Zeppelin. Malcolm Doney describes it as 'horrendous, heavy, mind-
deadening music . . . blacksmith music . . . a battering-
ram against the senses'.[18] Lemmy Kilminster of the
group Motorhead told *Hit Parader* that his group wanted
to see 'blood comin' out of everyone's ears, if possible.
Nothing dangerous, just enough to let us know they're
having a good time.'[19] As with repetition and beat, volume can have a 'hypnotic' effect – Doney writes of audiences who 'were only too willing to let themselves be
pushed along. They offered themselves up to the music.
They went to concerts with the specific intention of
being zonked out.'[20]

But *how loud is loud?* Sound level is measured in

decibels. In a paper entitled 'Hearing Acuity in Young People exposed to Pop Music and other Noise' Drs David Hanson and Ronald Fearn report that in visits to over thirty youth clubs they found average rock music decibel levels of between 84 and 118, with only one rating falling below 90.[21] At rock concerts, similar readings are common and can sometimes be in the 120-130 range. There have even been readings of 138 decibels. (As a working comparison, a vacuum cleaner generates about 80 decibels and a pneumatic hammer 94.)

Yet even these figures do not tell the whole story. Decibels increase *logarithmically*, not arithmetically, which means that an increase of only three decibels indicates *double* the intensity of sound. The standard British work on the subject of the effect of noise is *Hearing and Noise in Industry*, by Burns and Robinson, published by Her Majesty's Stationery Office. In it, they suggest that for an eight-hour working day, the maximum volume level should be 90 decibels, with the exposure duration being halved for every increase of three decibels.[22] This means that at 93 decibels the recommended maximum exposure should be four hours; for 96, two hours; for 99 one hour, and so on. Getting up to rock concert levels, the danger marks would be as follows: at 111 decibels, 3 minutes 45 seconds; at 120 decibels, 28.12 seconds; and at 129 decibels, 3.51 seconds. At the top recorded level we have mentioned (138 decibels) it would only be safe to listen for less than half a second!

With these figures in mind, it is not surprising to find that exposure to loud rock music has had serious effects on the hearing of the listeners. An ear, nose and throat specialist in the United States estimates that about 40% of students entering university have hearing defects caused by listening to rock music; twenty-five years ago, in pre-rock days, the figure was 1%. In a study carried out on 505 British students in higher education, Hanson and Fearn discovered that 'Statistically significant hearing losses were found in the group that admitted frequent attendance at pop music entertainment.'[23] Other studies by Ronald Fearn in the course of his work at Leeds Polytechnic suggested that up to one million young people in Britain suffered some degree of hearing loss caused by listening to loud music and that many have hearing problems normally associated with sixty-five to seventy-year-olds. No wonder Hanson and Fearn conclude their paper by calling overloud amplified music 'a widespread hazard'.[24]

It has been suggested to us that loudness in rock music is a matter of conditioning, but surely this is a highly dangerous philosophy? Should we allow ourselves to be conditioned by something that is potentially so harmful? Hanson and Fearn have the more obvious and sensible answer: 'The main requirement must be the reduction of amplification levels.'[25]

Yet quite apart from the sheer decibel level, there is another factor associated with volume that calls into question rock music's suitability as an evangelistic medium. Two very competent musicians, very much a part of the Christian pop scene, put it to us like this: 'The major problem of rock music is the noise level. The words are often inaudible and even if they were audible the degree of truth in them would be negligible. The whole scene has become a mess, with very many people not seeming to know why they are doing what they are doing.' That is a tragic commentary on the contemporary Christian music scene, made by people actively involved in it – and its most telling point is the one about the music making the words inaudible.

But in evangelism *the words are vitally important*. The Bible speaks of 'the *word* of truth, the gospel of your salvation' (Ephesians 1:13); it says that the gospel is 'the *word* of life' (Philippians 2:16); and that Christians are born again 'through the *word* of truth' (James 1:18). Then how can the work of evangelism be helped by something which makes its message more difficult to hear? In all the reasoning which we seek to bring to bear on our readers in this study of the use of rock music in evangelism, there is nothing on which we are more definite than this: any method or medium (we need not confine ourselves to rock music) which makes the gospel more difficult to hear, and therefore to be understood, *is not serving the cause of evangelism but actually hindering it*. The enthusiasm of the performers, the sincerity of their motives and the quality of their work may not be in question, but if at the end of the day the listeners cannot hear the *words* of the gospel then all of those qualities count for nothing.

The Christian music myth

If our analysis of rock music is right, using it in evangelism is spiritually perilous. But is it scripturally *possible*? Is there such a thing as 'Christian rock (or pop) music'? The way to begin answering that question is to ask a much more fundamental one, which is this: is there such a thing as 'Christian music' at all? What do we mean by the phrase? Are we describing the *music*? Take a sheet of music from a 'Christian song' and one from a 'secular song'. Are they essentially different? Is a B flat in a hymn any different from one in a bawdy rock number? Can you tell a Christian quaver from a non-Christian one? Is it something to do with the *instruments*? Is there such a thing as a godly guitar, a sanctified saxophone or a born-again bassoon? Nobody is questioning the point that one can have Christian musicians, but the simple fact of the matter is that *there is no such thing as 'Christian music'*. There are Christians and there is music; there is good music and there is bad music (and that statement has nothing to do with taste, style, culture or the age of the performer or listener); there is music that reflects God's glory and music that does not. We can take it further: there are Christians who write and play bad music, and non-Christians who write and play good music. Music is not 'good' because it is being performed in a religious context, any more than music is 'bad' because it is being performed in a 'secular' context. All these divisions tend to blur the truth. Music must be judged not by its context but by its content. Beautiful flowers can be found in a dusty desert and poisonous plants in a lovely garden.

How do we apply this principle? Man's first and constant duty is to honour his Maker in every area of his life – and that includes the most mundane things: 'So whether you eat or drink or whatever you do, do it all for the glory of God' (1 Corinthians 10:31). Every part of life is to be seen as one in which God can be glorified by our obedience to his revealed will. But this is not limited to 'religious' activities, let alone to evangelism. It is exactly here that so many people go wrong. As soon as a musician becomes a Christian he is encouraged to get involved in gospel music, because 'the Lord wants you to use your musical gift as a means of reaching other people with the gospel'. But who says so? Nowhere does the Bible tell the Christian that he must use whatever talents or means he has at his disposal as a vehicle for direct evangelism and its silence surely suggests that not all talents are appropriate for that purpose?

Lost property?

It has even been suggested to us that to question the rightness of using any particular kind of music in evangelism is to deny the lordship of Christ over part of his creation – but exactly the opposite is true. We deny his lordship when *we* decide that we can use any means we choose, then bring him in at the next stage and ask his blessing on it. But the musician's duty is the same as that of any other Christian – to begin with Scripture and dis-cover exactly what methods and means God has authorized. To imagine that by taking any kind of music (or other art form) and using it in direct evangelism we are somehow 'redeeming' or 'reclaiming' it for God is yet another popular piece of woolly thinking. According to Scripture, only believers' souls (now) and bodies (eventually) are *redeemed* by the blood of Christ; and God's plan 'to reconcile to himself all things' (Colossians 1:20) is something that he himself will bring to pass in 'a new heaven and a new earth, the home of righteousness' (2 Peter 3:13). The Christian is under no instruction or obligation to 'reclaim' art forms for God as if they were some kind of lost property.

Christians should be active in the arts, including music, but they do not have to drag the gospel into their art to make it biblically legitimate. A musician's first responsibility is to make *good* music, not *gospel* music – and the Lord will be glorified by the honesty, beauty and integrity of his work. As Professor H. R. Rookmaaker so perfectly puts it, 'Art has its own value,'[26] and that value is not tied to evangelism. The Christian artist (musician or other) need not feel trapped or confined to evangelism as a 'spiritual' expression of his art form. God has given him much greater liberty than that.

We shall presumably have to go on using phrases like 'Christian music', but it will help us to keep our thinking straight if we remember that there is really no such thing!

3.
Body language

In a report on the 1982 Greenbelt festival, *The Sunday Telegraph* contrasted Christianity's moral code with what it called 'the "sex 'n' drugs 'n' rock 'n' roll ethic"'.[1] The phrase may have been clumsy, but for many critics of the rock scene it probably said it all. They always knew that rock was rotten to the core, and when the good old *Sunday Telegraph* went on to speak of the apparent absurdity of 20,000 young Christians celebrating 'devil's music'[2] there were no doubt thousands of hearty 'Amens' (or at least 'Hear, hears') echoing around the land. If rock has its lovers, it also has its haters – and neither group has cornered the market on prejudice.

In the next three chapters we will turn from our very brief survey of rock music's history to take a close look at its up-to-date content and characteristics. We will not be short of material! Publicity is the staple diet of most rock performers, and their opinions, convictions, aims and philosophies are often public property. This means that the information and opinions come straight from the musical horses' mouths. It may not make pleasant reading, but it will certainly help to fill in the major pieces in the phenomenal musical jigsaw called rock.

Eros rules – OK?

One of the most persistent allegations about rock music

is that it has strong sexual connotations and can have adverse effects on the sexuality of those who listen to it. What is the evidence for this? Let us begin by calling in the technicians. In his book *Sound Effects, Youth Leisure and the Politics of Rock* Dr S. Frith reminds us that the impact of rock is generated primarily from the music's sound and rhythm, not its words. 'Rock is made', he says, 'in order to have emotional, social, physical, commercial results; it is not music made "for its own sake". Rock is in a sense primitive. It uses a primitive understanding of how sound effects and rhythms – prelinguistic devices – have their emotional and physical effects. Ignorance of how their music makes sense certainly puts no limit on a rock audience's appreciation. The response is to a large degree physical. *The rock experience is essentially erotic.*[3]

Drs Daniel and Bernadette Skubik, in a major study on the subject, say this: 'Rock music involves a neurophysiological conditioning in connotation or felt meaning, linking aggression and sexuality. Indeed, as rock music has moved farther away from its historical roots and medium (viz. folk music) *it both causes and expresses an increasing association of overt aggression linked with sexuality*. Psychological studies suggest that dominance, if not aggression, facilitates sexual arousal. The rock singer Linda Rondstadt, in an interview with Ron Rosenbaum (*Canberra Times* Magazine 20 October 1985) said, "Debasement and obstacles . . . is what love songs are about." According to Rondstadt, the purpose of rhythm is "to get you into an orgiastic state of losing yourself . . . I wish somebody would wire everybody with electrodes and take blood samples to demonstrate how powerfully the music affects body chemistry."' In the same work, the Skubiks say, 'Our basic claim is that the rock music itself induces a behavioural link between aggression and sexuality. J.L.Henry (1982) suggests that rock music could release endogenous endorphins, heightening the human sexual response.'[4] These findings raise wider issues concerning the neurophysiology of rock music, and these are discussed in the appendix.

Irwin Silber, spokesman for *Communist Causes in the USA* and Editor of *Sing Out,* has said that the great strength of rock lies in its beat and that it is music which is basically sexual and a threat to established patterns and values. It is not difficult to see why rock music has acquired this kind of reputation.

So much for the technicians; what about the performers? There can be no denying that from megastar Jimi Hendrix (who claimed to have slept with 1,000 women) onwards, many of its leading performers have made adultery, fornication, lesbianism, homosexuality or some other form of sexual deviation a way of life. Press reports of their sex lives have now become so common that they scarcely raise the readers' eyebrows. Yet we must be careful not to let this prejudice our views about their music. Sin of every kind is practised by people of every kind. No doubt there are dishonest dustmen, alcoholic accountants, perverted policemen and immoral ironmongers, but that does not mean that their offences are in any way related to their occupations. Nor are rock performers the only *musicians* to have murky morals – even some of the best-known classical composers were decidedly off-key in their private lives. Tchaikovsky was no paragon of virtue, Chopin had a reputation as a womanizer, Mahler was hardly blameless and Mozart's leisure haunts were not exactly havens of sanctity. As for Wagner, he has been described as 'grossly immoral, selfish, adulterous, arrogant, wildly hedonistic, violently racist and . . . a thief to boot'![5] These few examples will be sufficient to show that we need to be very careful before condemning any kind of artistic expression because of the life-style of those who write or perform it. If we took that line to its logical conclusion we would be living in a cultural desert.

We can go one step further and say that many classical compositions have murder, violence, hatred, greed, immorality or other evils as their themes and should be judged by the same standards as any other musical production. But the point at issue is whether we can single out rock music as having specifically sexual connotations – and the best place to begin is with the musicians and their performances.

Sex on stage

There is no denying the fact that, from Presley's twitching pelvis to the present day, sex has played a prominent part in the rock music scene, with the sexual temperature steadily rising. In 1977 *U.S. News and World Report* warned, 'Hot-selling songs with sexually explicit lyrics are moving up the charts, causing widespread concern about the effects on youth across the United States.'[6] Eleven years later *The Daily Telegraph* gave this assessment: 'Rock music has one appeal only, a barbaric appeal to sexual desire – not love, not *eros,* but sexual desire undeveloped and untutored.'[7] Today, compiling a list of those who blatantly mix sex with their songs almost calls for a computer. Here are some of the performers involved, listed in alphabetical order.

AC/DC (the name is deliberately bisexual) have a song which includes the words: 'Let me put my love into you, babe. Let me cut your cake with my knife.' In another song called 'You shook me all night long', the singer refers to a lover who 'took more than her share, had me fighting for air, working double time on my seduction line'.

David Bowie's bisexuality is such that at one stage he was voted Britain's number three male singer and number one female singer. Much of his material is depraved and vulgar.

Alice Cooper, preacher's son turned rock superstar, made a record called 'School's Out' which came wrapped in disposable ladies' panties. His song 'Muscle of Love' praises the pleasures of masturbation, while 'Welcome to my Nightmare' was staged by Alice simulating sex with a corpse.

Grand Funk's music (they sold up to ten million records a year) has been described as 'filled with sexual suggestion and power'.[8] Their manager is reported as saying, 'Listen man, what takes place on the stage of a rock concert doesn't happen spontaneously. It is carefully planned to elicit a sexual response from the audience,' and to have told the lead guitarist, 'Get out on stage and rape your guitar. That's what the girls want to see.'

Jimi Hendrix, the first black rock sex symbol in American pop music, drew this comment from Lillian Roxon: 'He does things to his guitar so passionate, so concentrated and intent that anyone with halfway decent manners has to look away.'[9]

Michael Jackson's film *Moonwalker* was released in the UK at the end of 1988. Cinema critic David Butler said that parts of it were 'stunning' and other parts 'crushingly twee and banal' and that these elements 'were all sandwiched among the wriggling, strutting, pouting striptease of the musical numbers, the androgynous figure, the face resculptured in its own image'.[10]

Jethro Tull's concerts have been described as 'bizarre

and loaded with sexualism',[11] with lead singer Ian Anderson talking about how his microphone 'has an erection'.[12]

KISS, who deliberately aim at the twelve to fifteen age group, and have a comic for nine to eleven-year-olds, concentrate heavily on sexual abuse and perversion. In the song 'Sweet Pain' they sing, 'My whip is ever beside me. Let me teach you love in a new and different way.' The group has been described by producer Bob Ezrin as 'symbols of unfettered evil and sensuality'.[13]

Led Zeppelin have a song called 'Trampled under Foot' in which they refer to a girl's 'transmission' flowing like hot oil while the singer says he would like to 'pump some gas'. In 'Whole Lotta Love' they sing, 'I'm gonna give you every inch of my love,' and the reference is crude and obvious.

Madonna's album 'Like a Virgin' is so sexually explicit that it was banned by many broadcasting agencies, yet at one stage it sold over three million copies in fourteen weeks. She is quoted as saying, 'Crucifixes are sexy because there is a naked man on them.'[14]

Meat Loaf drew this comment from a teenager in a letter to *New Musical Express:* 'I have just walked out of a Meat Loaf concert. I was absolutely disgusted by the way Meat Loaf and the female vocalists were acting. Why didn't they just strip off, get down on the floor and have sex? That's what the audience would have loved.'

Pink Floyd's album 'The Wall' was voted by *Rolling Stone* as the No. 1 album of the year; it included the lyrics, 'Oh, I need a dirty woman, Oh, I need a dirty girl!'

Prince rated a feature in *Newsweek* entitled 'The Naughty Prince of Rock,' which said, 'He's a prophet of sexual anarchy: his X-rated act has made him a new-wave cult hero and a huge hit with black ghetto youth . . . Prince's apparent religious belief in salvation through sex makes him unique . . . His current road show is a razzle-dazzle riot of erotic funk.'[15] In a song entitled 'Sexuality' he sings, 'It's the Second Coming, anything goes!' Music magazine *Rolling Stone* said of one of his LPs (for which Prince wrote, produced and played all the instruments), 'Nothing could have prepared us for the liberating lewdness of "Dirty Mind". At its best it is positively filthy. Sex, with its lasting urges and temporary satisfaction, holds a fascination that drives the singer to extremes of ribald fantasy.'[16]

Queen (another name with sexual hints) made a smash hit with 'We are the Champions', which has been described as 'an anthem of gay liberation'.[17] Lead singer Freddie Mercury, who cranks up the group's bisexual image by wearing mascara, nail varnish and hot pants, admits, 'We want to shock and be outrageous.'[18]

The *Rolling Stones'* typical presentation has been called 'an orgy of sexual celebration, with Jagger as the head cheerleader'.[19] Their song 'Sweet Virginia' includes the line, 'I gave you diamonds, you gave me disease' (a reference to venereal disease). The cover of their album 'Sticky Fingers' came with a real zip; underneath was a picture of a thinly covered male crotch.

Rod Stewart sings 'Tonight's the Night' and invites his angelic virgin lover to spread her wings so that he can 'come inside'. He first hit stardom with 'Maggie May', which includes the lyrics, 'Oh, mother, what a lover!

You wore me out, wrecked my bed, and in the morning kicked me in the head.' He told *Hit Parader,* 'We had an amazing experience the other night. At one point I had about fifteen brassieres around my waist. I've never seen so many brassieres thrown up on stage – they just kept coming and I stuck them in my trousers. I had them all around – that was a really good concert!'[20]

Shakin' Stevens was once headlined as 'the New King of Rock' in the *Daily Mirror.* Reporting on his concert, the paper said, 'Halfway through the performance the atmosphere sweats with buttoned-down sexual excitement cascading over the guy on the stage, who does things with the microphone as sexually explicit as the law allows.'[21]

Sting produced this assessment in the *Daily Express:* 'He has a kind of aura . . . the eyes and the look ... The sexiest image in rock.'[22]

Tina Turner was described in *Newsweek* as 'the sexy godmother of rock',[23] while another writer called her 'the high priestess of "raunch and roll" . . . the one who wears lingerie on stage most women wouldn't wear to bed'.[24]

The *Who* drew this comment from Tony Palmer: 'They have a direct sexual impact. They ask a question – "Do you want to, or don't you?" And they don't really give the audience a chance of saying "No". It's a sort of rape.'[25]

These examples are no more than that and we have deliberately omitted many more that are too disgusting and revolting to include. To a greater or lesser degree, dozens of other top rock groups and hundreds of minor ones show the same blatantly sexual orientation. But does that prove that rock is nothing more than musical sex?

Fact or fantasy?

One of the dangers arising from the publicity given to rock stars is that we end up believing what we see and hear. But that is about as clever as believing everything claimed by television commercials. The point is well made by Steve Lawhead: 'Since rock musicians are image manipulators, most often what they say and do is calculated for a purpose. Usually that purpose is attention.'[26] He gives Alice Cooper as an example and writes, 'Alice Cooper is fairly well known for his shocking stage performances – such as beheadings, cavorting with live snakes, hangings, surrealistic nightmare sequences. But Vincent Furier (Alice's real name) does not sit around at home wearing torn leotards and grotesque facial make-up. According to numerous interviews, he plays golf and softball, watches television and goes about his life much the same as anyone else. His life off stage is dull compared to what he projects in the spotlight.'[27] Malcolm Doney agrees. He calls Alice Cooper's activities 'the product of a crass commercialism',[28] and says that 'The decadent image of David Bowie and Lou Reed was part of the same game-playing mentality.'[29]

No doubt the illusion is widespread. Elton John once said 'There is nothing wrong in going to bed with somebody of your own sex. I think people should be very free with sex – they should draw the line at goats.'[30] Of course it produced widespread publicity – but was it *serious*? Separating fact from fantasy in this area is not easy, but this does not make dirty lyrics, obscene gestures and deviant sexual claims any more acceptable, nor does it lessen their impact on the morals of the listeners.

The filth connection

The mucky picture we have painted would explain why a leading rock magazine can refer to 'prophylactic rock'[31] and why Bob Larson can speak of tunes known in the industry as 'masturbatory rock'.[32] But is that how the performers see it? It is one thing to act out sexual fantasies to music, but what is their *philosophy* of rock? Do they see any connection between rock and sex? Here, without comment, are the views of some of those in the upper reaches of the rock music scene.

Johnny Bristol: 'Sex is where it's at in music . . . and I like it.'[33]

Duran Duran: 'You've got to be pretty sexless to hold a guitar, dance with it on stage and not put over some kind of sexuality.'[34] John Taylor, the group's bassist, once said, 'When the music works, the audience and the performer often feel like they're having an orgasm together.'[35]

Glenn Frey of the Eagles: 'I'm in rock music for the sex and narcotics.'[36]

Mick Jagger: 'You can feel the adrenalin flowing through your body. It's sort of sexual. I entice my audience. What I do is very much the same as a girl's striptease dance.'[37] 'Sometimes, being on stage is better than an orgasm.'[38]

Punk rock manager *Malcolm McLaren* said, 'Rock 'n' roll is pagan and primitive, and very jungle, and that's how it should be! The moment it stops being those things, it's dead . . . That's what rock 'n' roll is meant to be about, isn't it? . . . the true meaning of rock . . . is sex, subversion and style.'[39]

Freddie Mercury of the group Queen: 'I do deliver sex appeal. It's part of modern rock. I sell sex appeal with my body movements on stage.'[40]

Jim Morrison: 'I feel spiritual up there. Think of us as erotic politicians.'[41]

Ted Nugent: 'I've sold over fifteen million records so far, but I'm not in it for the money. I do this for the excitement and the girls I can get.'[42]

John Oates: 'Rock 'n' roll is 99% sex.'[43]

Richard Oldham, manager of the Rolling Stones: 'Rock music is sex and you have to hit them [teenagers] in the face with it.'[44]

Jimmy Page of Led Zeppelin: 'Rock 'n' roll is sexually — you music.'[45]

Whitesnake's lead singer: 'Let's face it – rock 'n' roll is all about making love.'[46]

Frank Zappa, superstar of Mothers of Invention fame: 'Rock music is sex. The big beat matches the body's rhythms.'[47]

These comments are more serious than those we quoted a little earlier, as they have less obvious publicity value. They may therefore take us a little closer to the truth –

and what the people concerned are saying is that there is
a very definite connection between sex and the music in
which they are involved. Have they *all* got it wrong?

What's in a name?

To anyone dropping into today's pop music scene from,
say, a hundred years back, even the terminology we use
would be totally incomprehensible. How could we possibly explain to them that 'punk' and 'funk' are variations
of 'rock'? What would 'rock' mean to them? Even more
to the point, what does it mean to us? As we have seen,
'rock' is a post-Beatle refinement of 'rock 'n' roll' – but
what does 'rock 'n' roll' *mean*? What has it got to do with
a particular musical style? Where did the name come
from? How did it get used to describe the music it does?
    The phrase itself seems to have been born in the
American black ghetto communities at the end of the
Second World War, where it was a slang phrase for fornication. As such, it soon found its way into the very
earthy rhythm-and-blues songs of the time. In 1951 Alan
Freed, a disc jockey in Cleveland, Ohio, was looking for
a phrase to describe the growing spill-over of rhythm-
and-blues music, which he was beginning to play on his
white radio station, a phrase that would capture the
spirit of the music and mirror the growing excitement it
was generating among young people. The phrase he
chose was 'rock 'n' roll'. It has been said that Freed
chose the phrase to make the music more acceptable to
white listeners. That may well be the case, but that was
not why it was originally coined and his choice may have
been more significant than he realized. One thing is certain, the sexual connotation remained; the fear of many
is that it fits the music too well to be merely coincidental.

Not the last word

The secular press can never be accused of undue bias in favour of biblical standards, nor of being overly prissy about morality in general. It is interesting, therefore, to read the following comments on the subject of sex and rock.

Time magazine once observed that 'In a sense all rock is revolutionary. By its very beat and sound it has always implicitly rejected restraints and has celebrated freedom and sexuality.'[48] *Newsweek's* Robert Hilburn added, 'Disco is a temporary thrill – a night in a bordello.'[49]

Herbert Kretzmer, television critic of the *Daily Mail,* wrote that 'Songs, in short, have become the new pornography. Only the deaf, uncaring or wholly distracted will fail to notice this.' Peggy Chrimes, the *Daily Mirror's* television critic, writing about the tendency to screen rock programmes earlier in the evening, complained, 'It is a ready-made excuse to take the sex out of rock 'n' roll, which is a pity, because that's what it's all about.'[50] The *Daily Mail's* Lynda Lee-Potter wrote an article about the dangerous sexual pressures being brought to bear on young girls, in which she commented, 'The entire pop world is geared to titillating the young, in arousing children to frenzied ecstasy as erotically dressed pop stars scream invitations to sexual behaviour far beyond their audience's years.'[51]

Jazz musician and entertainer George Melly has no doubts about the sexual impact of certain kinds of music. In his book *Revolt into Style* he writes, 'The effect of a top pop group on an audience of pubescent girls is clearly masturbatorial.'[52] Later he adds this: 'The pop idol is transformed into a masturbation fantasy object for adolescent girls. The shrieking, squirming audience is in the process of self-induced mass orgasm. Not all girls are prepared to leave it at fantasy level. Some are so stimulated that they are prepared to make do with any-one even tentatively connected with the group, as many a middle-aged manager or young band boy will substantiate.'[53]

This particular feature of rock is a nauseating fulfil-ment of something prophesied as long ago as 1965 by Jan Berry of *Jan and Dean,* who said, 'The throbbing beat of rock-and-roll provides a vital sexual release for its ado-lescent audience,' and suggested that 'The next big trend in rock-and-roll will be to relieve the sexual tensions of the pre-adolescent set.'

All of these statements coincide exactly with those of the rock musicians we quoted earlier, and many obser-vers of the social scene have come to the same conclu-sion. At an annual Headmasters' Conference, repre-senting over 200 public schools, the Rev. Professor Moelwyn Merchant told his audience, 'I think explicit sex is much less dangerous than the plugging of pop records that lower the whole tone of human relation-ships . . .It is the disc jockeys and their plugging of debased sensory material and the debasement of images who are the real pornographers.'[54] Viewing things from quite a different angle, television personality David Frost described BBC TV's *Top of the Pops* as 'sex to music, when young people go through the motions of going to bed without actually doing so'. Author David A. Noebel was just as succinct: 'Rock 'n' roll is musical pornography.'[55]

The argument about the relationship between sex and rock goes on. Even Steve Lawhead (who is by no means 'anti-rock') admits, 'There is more blatant immorality being peddled in popular music now than ever before.'[56] But is rock a cause of today's immoral ethic or just a car-rier? Exactly how much blame should it carry? Do we indict it or excuse it? Christians must make up their own minds on the evidence they have, relating that evidence at all times to the clear teaching of Scripture. But there is another important question: can we use rock music without any danger of getting tainted by its immoral associations? Richard Taylor, author of *A Return to Christian Culture,* is in no doubt about the answer: 'We cannot foster an erotic type of music and expect to succeed in avoiding the erosion of standards and ideals. Rock music has a message and it is the message of sexual permissiveness. As music affects your body you instinctively want to put motions to it. So what kind of motions fit rock music? Basically sensual motions. If the message of rock music produces that sort of response, then it is not good music for a Christian.'[57]

Analysing the current British scene, a contemporary Christian youth magazine said, 'Even the most vocal supporters of rock and pop would admit that there is much in the scene to disturb any Christian conscience. A *large percentage of pop hits* contain in their lyrics blatantly un-Christian morality, ranging from casual acceptance of sex before marriage to the unspeakably pornographic (witness Haysi Fantayzee on BBC TV's *Top of the Pops*).'[58] Later in the same article it spoke of a 'tidal wave of songs celebrating young lust', of Satanism being an 'in vogue image for heavy rock bands' and of 'rackfuls of sub-Christian filth available in Britain's high street record shops'.[59]

Yet this is part of the daily diet of many young Christians, who are not enthusiastic about gospel rock only, but addicted to pop music in general. Many presumably have no idea of the mental, emotional and spiritual conflicts that are being set up, but as Bob Larson comments, 'A mind that has been infiltrated by lyrical pornography throughout the week cannot easily be remoulded with only a few hours allotted for Christian instruction on Sunday.'[60]

Nearly 2,000 years ago the apostle Paul gave the seven-days-a-week solution: 'Let us purify ourselves from everything that contaminates body and spirit, perfecting holiness out of reverence for God' (2 Corinthians 7:1). Fifteen centuries later, Martin Luther keyed Paul's words in to the music scene of his own day: 'I wish that the young men might have something to rid them of their love ditties and wanton songs and might instead of these learn wholesome things and thus yield willingly to the good; also because I am not of the opinion that all the arts shall be crushed to earth and perish through the gospel, as some bigoted persons pretend, but would willingly see them all, and especially music, servants of him who gave and created them.'[61]

For many young Christians, Luther's application of the Bible's principles would mean a transformation of their musical tastes. It might also call for a bonfire!

4.
Strange fire

A second major reason why its strongest critics allege that rock music is unsuitable for Christian use is that it has close links with the occult. It has been said that 'Any fusion of secular methods with sacred intentions is in danger of becoming a truce with the world.'[1] If rock's connection with the occult can be proved, then its fusion with the Christian faith would be absurd as well as dangerous. It would not merely be a truce with the world but with the *underworld,* and 'What do righteousness and wickedness have in common? Or what fellowship can light have with darkness?' (2 Corinthians 6:14).

Dark world

The word 'occult' means 'hidden, secret, supernatural', but we must not let those vague words fool us and hide the fact that the occult world is real and menacing. One of Satan's most successful tactics has been to convince people that he does not exist, that he and his agents are just figments of man's religious imagination. Yet no Christian should fall for that. The Bible teems with references to him, and always as a real and living being who is brilliant and intelligent and staggeringly power-ful; the Bible even goes so far as to call him 'the god of this age' (2 Corinthians 4:4). What is more, he is in vicious and bitter opposition to everything that is good, wholesome, pure and righteous. The very word 'Satan' means 'adversary' or 'opponent', and as Dr Leon Morris says, 'Satan is a malignant reality, always hostile to God and to God's people.'[2]

The Bible is equally clear about the existence of Satan's countless agents, which it refers to as 'demons', 'devils' and 'evil spirits'. We read of them oppressing some people, possessing others. They have the power to bring about physical, mental and spiritual disorder, as well as to cause their victims to be gripped by sin of one kind or another.

One of the greatest powers possessed by Satan and his agents is their ability to appear harmless, benign, or even helpful. The Bible says that there are times when Satan 'masquerades as an angel of light' (2 Corinthians 11:14) – and this must surely be one of the reasons why this dark, sinister world has so much fascination for many people. The Spiritualists' Association of Great Britain speaks of the greatest upsurge of interest in spiritualism since Victorian days. An occult book club has attracted over one million members. Large sections of libraries and bookshops are given over to the subject. There may be as many as 45,000 witches operating in Britain alone. Horoscopes appear in over 1,000 of our newspapers and magazines, while both BBC and ITV have screened programmes featuring astrologers as part of the 'entertainment'. One of the biggest challenges facing the Christian church today is the fact that thousands of people are interested in the supernatural but rarely, if ever, associate it with the ministry of the church!

Ignorance iceberg

As one would expect, Satan and his forces have deeply

invaded man's social and cultural situations, and music has not been left out. Read these chilling words by the manager of one of the biggest rock bands in the world: 'If you study rock you'll see it has gone through four phases, each one appealing to one side of the human personality. In the late nineteen-fifties and early nineteen-sixties we appealed almost entirely to sex. In the late nineteen-sixties and early nineteen-seventies, we moved young people into a new area of consciousness in terms of their spirit. We got them involved in causes. It was then that drugs became a primary association with the rock culture. In the late nineteen-seventies we moved them into an addictive form of punk rock or new wave. The music was not really predicated on talent, but mainly we were trying to create an addiction to violence . . . Now we discovered the best motivation there is to buy a product. The best motivation in the world is religious commitment. No human being ever makes a deeper commitment than a religious commitment, so we decided that in the nineteen-eighties we are going to have religious services in our concerts. We are going to pronounce ourselves as Messiahs. We are going to make intimate acquaintances and covenants with Satan . . . and we will be worshipped.'[3]

That whole statement is frightening. Notice the phrases, 'we moved young people', and 'we moved them'. So much for the argument that music is neutral! But the most frightening thing is the one that speaks of deliberate association with Satan.

One of the people with whom we discussed the whole subject of rock music and evangelism is a highly qualified Christian musician who writes, arranges, performs and teaches music from the classics to rock. In a private paper he wrote, 'There is no disputing that satanic and occult connections occur in the rock world . . . this is a spiritual minefield and it is right that you should be concerned that many Christians are ignorant of these matters.' Dave Roberts, writing one of a series of open letters in *Buzz* (a Christian youth magazine now superseded by *21st Century Christian)* warns naïve readers, 'I'll bet you aren't aware of all the occultic propaganda in your record collections,'[4] and in the introduction to the feature, *Buzz* admits that 'Vinyl blasphemies sit proudly in the records of many unaware Christians.'[5]

How widespread is the ignorance? We can certainly give many examples from our own observation and experience. We have seen young Christians wearing T-shirts advertising groups heavily into occultism. A record shop owned by Christians had a large central display promoting a Black Sabbath album entitled 'Live Evil'. At an evangelical church we found the youth leader playing 'Bat out of Hell' by Meat Loaf while preparing the church hall for that night's coffee bar; he was amazed when we told him of the group's occultic connections and said that he had been playing the album all afternoon – it was one of his favourites! At another church we had a limited opportunity to speak on rock music and the gospel. As soon as we got back to our 'digs' our host went to his record collection, picked out a fistful of albums and said, 'These will have to go. I had no idea these groups were into the occult.'

We are sure that this is just the tip of an 'ignorance iceberg' and that thousands of young Christians are unknowingly supporting the work of rock musicians whose beliefs and practices they would find frightening and revolting.

Check those decks!

However cautious we may have to be in some other

areas of the rock music debate, this is at least one in which we must be clear, definite and decisive. Here, in alphabetical order, is a list of rock musicians whose life-styles or music show occultic influence of one kind or another.

AC/DC. A hallmark of their albums is the satanic 'S'. Their album 'Back in Black' has a song entitled 'Hell's Bells', including the words 'Satan's gonna get you'. The cover of the album 'Highway to Hell' shows a member with horns and another wearing a pentagram (a satanic symbol). The title song includes the words, 'I'm on my way to the promised land, I'm on the highway to hell.'

Alice Cooper. In a story syndicated in the American national press, he told how (as Vincent Furier) he attended a seance at which a spirit was conjured and promised him and his band world-wide success if he would change his name to that of the spirit (Alice Cooper) and allow the spirit to possess his body. During an appearance on the *Muppet Show*, fun was made of his demon possession.

Ginger Baker, thought by many to be the top rock drum-mer in the world. Asked about his emotional feelings when drumming, he replied, 'It happens to us quite often – it feels as though I'm not playing my instrument, something else is playing it and that same thing is playing all three of our instruments' (a reference at that time to the Cream). 'That's what I mean when I say it's frighten-ing sometimes.'[6]

Chuck Berry. Time asked, 'Why shouldn't the father of the fifties rock 'n' roll look like every white kid's slumber-party dream of Satan? A slim body, supple as sin, wavy hair, drenched in Valvoline and just full enough to hide those tell-tale horns.'[7]

The Beach Boys. Dennis Wilson had links with the notorious Manson family; Mike Love and Al Jardine were into Transcendental Meditation. Bob Larson claims that 'The fame of the Beach Boys was a launching pad for the Maharishi Mahesh Yogi's introduction of TM and occultic mysticism into the mainstream of America.'[8]

Black Sabbath. The name of the group refers to an occultic ritual and they have been known to introduce their concerts by holding black masses on stage, complete with a nude on an altar sprinkled with chicken blood. Their first album, 'Black Sabbath', pictured a witch on the front. Group member Bill Ward says, 'Satan could be God,'[9] while Geezer, the bass player, claims he is the seventh son of a seventh son, is Lucifer, and can see the devil: 'It's a satanic world.'[10] Lead singer Ozzie Osbourne claims he was compelled to see the film *The Exorcist* twenty-six times, and on another occasion said, 'The devil is within us all the time. It's here. All this is the devil.'[11] Several members of the group admit to astral projection. Their albums include 'We sold our souls for rock and roll', with the cover featuring the satanic 'S', and 'Sabbath, Bloody Sabbath', with the cover showing a nude satanic ritual emblazoned with the number 666 (the Bible's description of the Antichrist). Included in their promotional paraphernalia is a bumper sticker with the words: 'I am possessed by Black Sabbath.'

David Bowie. In an interview with *Rolling Stone* he said, 'Rock has always been the devil's music. You can't convince me that it isn't. I honestly believe everything that

I've said. I believe that rock 'n' roll is dangerous.'[12] At
one point in his career it was reported that he drew pen-
tagrams (satanic symbols) on his walls and made hexes
(other satanic devices) while burning candles.[13]

Blue Oyster Cult. Their symbol is that of the mythological child-eating god Kronos. All of their albums feature
the satanic cross (an upside-down question mark in the
cross of Christ, questioning the deity of God). The cover
of the album 'Agents of Fortune' shows a magician holding tarot cards with the message that he who comes
against the power faces death.

Chris De Burgh mixes blasphemy and occultism. The
cover of his album 'Chris De Burgh Live in S.A.'
includes the Christian cross and an inverted red cross – a
satanic symbol. His song 'Spanish Train' ends with the
words, 'The devil still cheats and wins more souls. As for
the Lord, well, he's just doing his best.'[14]

Deep Purple. The group is said to have recorded at least
one album in a seventeenth-century castle supposedly
haunted by a demon who is a servant of the Babylonian
god Baal.

The Eagles. Now disbanded, the group took its name
from the chief spirit in the Indian cosmos[15] and the group
was formed under the occultic influence of Carlos Cas-
taneda. They admit to writing most of their songs while
under the influence of the drug peyote. Several of their
songs, such as 'Witchy Woman', 'One of these Nights'
and 'Good Day in Hell', include satanic or occultic
lyrics. One of their songs, 'Undercover Angel', speaks
about having sexual intercourse with evil spirits and one
of their albums bears the goat's head insignia (an occultic symbol).

Earth, Wind and Fire. The group's name comes from the three major elements in the cosmos. Their song 'Serpentine Fire' speaks of the sinal life entity system found in the Shah Krishna Yogi Meditation Cult. On the American television show *20/20* on 15 January 1981 they were filmed in the home of a member of the group which was full of Eastern gods and occultic symbols. On the programme, they claimed to 'have an interest in Eastern religion, astrology, numerology and the occult'. Lead singer Maurice White believes that he possesses powers from previous incarnations and has the group join hands in a circle before beginning a show, so as to tune in to the force of the 'higher powers'.[16]

Fleetwood Mac. The group had a hit called 'Rhiannon' which was dedicated to a Welsh witch.[17] Lead singer Stevie Nicks sometimes dedicates songs in a concert to 'all the witches of the world'. Their satanic leanings come through in the song 'Gold Dust Woman', while the closing lyrics of another song are 'Hail, great shadow of demon, great shadow of dragon'.

Steve Hackett, guitarist with the group Genesis.[18] He recorded a solo album entitled 'Voyage of the Acolyte' with songs based on his musical interpretation of the tarot cards.

George Harrison. In his days with the Beatles, Harrison was one of the first to turn their thoughts to the teachings of Maharishi Mahesh Yogi. He subsequently became a devotee of Hinduism and a powerful advertisement for TM. His smash-hit song 'My Sweet Lord' (which was accepted by many Christians) is a song of dedication to the Hindu god Vishnu and contains a chant of calling forth the spirits of Krishna consciousness. His albums include a number of other songs promoting Hinduism.

Jimi Hendrix. Before his death Jimi Hendrix was heavily involved in the demonic supernatural. He wore a medicine shirt from a Hopi reservation and claimed that he had come from an asteroid belt off the coast of Mars. He also claimed to have seen UFOs filling the skies above the Woodstock rock festival.[19] Hindu gods were featured on the cover of his album 'Axis: Bold as Love'. He openly admitted that he had visions and communed with spirits.[20]

Michael Jackson's video promoting his song 'Torture' has been described as 'occultic to the core'.[21]

Elton John's lyricist, Bernie Taupin, told *People* Magazine that he decorates his walls with 'satanic art' and admitted, 'The occult fascinates me.'[22]

Iron Maiden. The title track of their album 'The Number of the Beast' (advertised as being 'forged in the fires of hell') is a song called '666'. The opening track, 'Moonchild', is supposedly sung by the devil. In a later album, 'Seventh Son of a Seventh Son' the son concerned is a clairvoyant. Iron Maiden has come under fire for making more satanic music than almost any other band. Many of their songs refer to the Antichrist; most of the lyrics are obsessed with hellish imagery, and seven out of eight songs on one album alone pertain to themes of death and assorted evils.[23] Lead singer Bruce Dickinson admitted that during the recording of the album a succession of things went wrong, including an accident involving producer Martin Birch's car which produced a repair bill for £666.56. Dickinson admitted, 'That was just too close for comfort. he was absolutely terrified and the rest of us were very shaken.'[24]

KISS. One-time drummer Peter Criss is reported as saying, 'I find myself evil. I believe in the devil as much as I believe in God. You can use either one to get things done.' During their concerts they breathe fire, levitate their instruments and regurgitate blood. Their album covers bear the satanic 'S'. Their song 'God of Thunder' includes the words: 'I gather darkness to please me and I command you to kneel before the god of thunder and rock 'n' roll.'

Kissing Bandits were so taken up by the work of artist-cum-witch Una Woodruffe that they asked her to design the sleeve of their début single, 'Shake some action!' The witch obliged by weaving a spell into her artwork.

Led Zeppelin. On the inside cover of their album 'House of the Holy' is a picture of a naked man holding up a child in sacrifice to a mysterious light on the top of a ruined building. The cover of 'Presence' shows a strange object which guitarist Jimmy Page says symbolizes the force that enables the group to have such power over audiences, a power known only as a 'presence'. Page bought a house once belonging to the infamous British spiritualist, murderer and sexual pervert Aleister Crowley (who renamed himself 'The Beast 666')[25] and now runs Equinox, Britain's largest occult bookshop.

John McLaughlin, guitar virtuoso of the now disbanded Mahavishnu Orchestra. A convert to Hinduism, McLaughlin is devoted to his guru, Sri Chinmoy. He claims that 'Through the grace of Sri Chinmoy I have become more aware of the real presence of the Supreme

Being',[26] and told *Newsweek*, 'When I let the spirit play me, it's an intense delight.'[27]

Meat Loaf. Their album cover for 'Bat out of Hell' features a demon and speaks of a mutant motorcyclist riding out of the pit of hell. The group's leader is reported as saying, 'When I go on stage, I get possessed.'[28] Their composer Jim Steinman said, 'I've always been fascinated by the supernatural and always felt rock was the perfect idiom for it.'[29]

Moody Blues: Their album 'In Search of the Lost Chord' speaks about a musical chord with supernatural properties. The inside of the album cover has a 'yantra' (the visual equivalent of a mantra in TM). There are also instructions to the listener to stare at the geometric designs while the music is being played, in order to enter an altered state of consciousness. The title of one track on the record is 'OM', a Hindu Sanskrit word used for God, in which he is thought to be embodied in the very word itself.

Motorhead's logo is a vicious-looking skull with fangs and goat's horns protruding from the mouth, and the group has produced songs such as 'Dancing on your Grave'.

Van Morrison. He claims that he experienced a spiritual transformation through reading literature on Celtic witchcraft history and the supernatural.[30]

Nazareth. Their album 'Hair of the Dog' has demonic manifestations on the cover.

Queen. The lyrics of 'Bohemian Rhapsody' include the statement that Beelzebub has a devil set aside for them.

Rainbow. Leader Ritchie Blackmore has been called one of the foremost rock occultists and admits that he regularly holds seances 'to get closer to God'. He also claims that when on stage he indulges in astral-projection, hovering above the concert hall.[31]

The *Rolling Stones*. Group member Keith Richards once said, 'There are black magicians who think we are acting as unknown agents of Lucifer and others who think we are Lucifer.'[32] *Newsweek* once called Mick Jagger 'the Lucifer of rock, the unholy roller', and spoke of 'his demonic power to affect people'.[33] On the cover of one of their earlier albums 'Their Satanic Majesties Request', the Stones dressed up as male witches. Their song 'Sympathy for the Devil' has become an unofficial anthem for Satanists. Part of their album 'Goat's Head Soup' was recorded at a voodoo ritual and the track includes the screams of those being possessed by evil spirits. The album cover design includes a colour picture of a goat's head (a satanic symbol) floating in a boiling cauldron. One of the songs is 'Dancing with Mr D' and is about a midnight dance with the devil in a graveyard.

Rush. Their album 'Caress of Steel' has a cover design featuring a robed man levitating a pyramid. Most of their albums have a pentagram on the cover. They perform in front of a pentagram on stage.

Santana. Group leader Carlos Santana has said, 'I am the strong and the Supreme is the musician. When I'm really in tune with the Supreme, my guru and my instrument, forget it man, 'cause it's totally beyond anything. That's where I want to be.' Two of the group's albums portray a lion's head; one is made up of human faces and the other of serpents, idols and roses. They have an album entitled 'Abraxas', the name of a leading demon spirit. Songs on the album include 'Black Magic Woman' and 'Evil Ways'.

The *Strawbs*. Their song 'Brave New World' contains a quotation from Buddha as well as a prayer to Ra, the Egyptian sun god.

Styx. The group's name comes from the mythological river that is supposed to run through hell. Their album 'Cornerstone' includes the song 'We've found it'. The reference is to the cornerstone of the Great Pyramid – but the Great Pyramid does not have a cornerstone; that is reserved for the pyramid's deity, Lucifer.

Tangerine Dream. William Friedkin, director of the film *The Exorcist*, claims that this group's music inspired his film *The Sorcerer*.

Toyah. She has spoken openly about her occultic experiences as a child.[34]

Uriah Heep. Their album 'Demons and Wizards' features a variety of occultic songs including 'Traveller in Time', about astral projection. 'The Magician's Birthday' also has reference to the occult.

Utopia. Group leader Tod Rundgren admits to believing in astral projection and reincarnation,[35] and that lyrics for many of their songs are based on Japanese and Egyptian mysticism.[36] Rundgren's album 'Ra' is dedicated to the Egyptian sun god and his guitar is in the shape of an ankh (a symbol of lust and fertility). Stage props for Utopia include a twenty-five-foot gold pyramid.

Venom. The members of the group 'proudly declare that

they feel possessed before they go on stage' and their songs are saturated with occultic themes.[37]

White Witch. One of their album cover designs is in the shape of an ankh. They major in 'white magic' of which Anton LaVey, priest of the First Church of Satan in California said, 'Call it black, call it white, call it what you will. It's all evil and it all gets its power from the source of evil.'

The *Who*. The leader of this group is Peter Townshend, who follows the teachings of Meher Baba, an Eastern metaphysical guru. Townshend put out a solo album which included a Hindu prayer and declared that 'Baba is Christ.' Tony Palmer says that when they play 'there is a distinct feeling of the presence of evil'.[38]

Stevie Wonder. His album 'Songs in the Key of Life' was released to coincide with his astrological birth-sign Taurus.[39] The album cover for 'Inner Visions' depicts the symbol of astral projection.

Yes. The group's album 'Tales from Topographic Oceans' contains songs said to reveal the science of God, tantric sexual rituals and reincarnation.

That catalogue is both sickening and frightening and there is no telling how many other bands, singers and musicians may be involved in the occult and whose music may be impregnated with the poison.

For example, *Newsweek* questioned songs like 'Billie Jean', 'Beat it', 'Wanna be Startin' Something', and 'Thriller', all huge hits for megastar Michael Jackson: 'Each one is quirky, strange, deeply personal, with offbeat lyrics that hint at Michael's own secret world of dreams and demons.'[40]

For *Buzz* blithely to assure its readers that the issue is limited to 'an occasional rock singer . . . dabbling with the occult'[41] is dangerously naive.

Symbols of Satan

One of Britain's best-known witches is Sybil Leek. In her book *Numerology* she claims that 'Many rock musicians cast spells and incantations upon their music, and then to demonstrate that they have made a pact with the devil they place occultic symbols on their record sleeves. Such symbols include crystal balls, goats' heads, upside down crosses, tarot card characters, pyramids, 2/4, palmistry signs of the Zodiac, the satanic ass, a five-pointed star in a circle, the extended tongue and the "Il Cornuto" sign'.[42] The latter is a traditional Sicilian sign (forefinger and little finger extended, other fingers curled into a fist) used among black arts practitioners to ward off 'the evil eye'. As far as we can tell, the Beatles were the first to use this on a record sleeve; it can be seen clearly on the cover of their album 'Yellow Submarine'.

Leek's statements about the widespread use of occultic symbols can easily be confirmed by glancing at the shelves of the average secular record store. Satan is big business; as Mick Jagger calmly admitted, 'Satanism sells records.'[43]

In the grooves

In addition to all of this, there is the controversial subject of subliminal messages inserted at slow speed, 'super-speed' or by backward masking, a device by which material is inserted in such a way that it only becomes intelligible when played backwards.

The concept is frightening, particularly as there is scientific evidence that subliminal messages can be received, stored, unscrambled and impressed on the mind *without the knowledge of the listener*. Dr Wilson Bryan Key, who has done extensive research on the subject, says, 'All subliminals are purposefully designed with the motive of soliciting, manipulating, modifying or managing human behaviour.'[44] Elsewhere he wrote, 'The unconscious system appears to be able to unscramble even certain kinds of distorted information without individuals becoming consciously aware of the perception.'[45] Along the same lines, he also wrote, 'Anything consciously perceived can be evaluated, criticized, discussed, argued and possibly rejected, whereas unconsciously perceived information *meets no resistance or qualification by the intellect.*'[46] Dr Key's conclusions are endorsed by Dr Lloyd Silverman, Professor of Psychology at New York University: 'There are two brain centres that deal with outside stimuli. The one centre is responsible for registering a stimulus, the other for bringing it into consciousness. The first centre is far more sensitive than the second, so that a very weak stimulus (such as low volume words hidden below the music, or inserted backwards) will register in the mind *but won't come into the consciousness.*'[47] In simple terms, this means that material inserted by backward masking is not 'lost', but is readily accessible to the listener *without his knowing that this is the case*. As an article in *Newsweek* put it, 'The brain seems able to handle backward-masking images with ease. Document forgers have used this technique for years.'[48]

It might be useful at this point to list the three main categories of subliminals.

The first consists of pictures or words flashed up very quickly on to a cinema or television screen – so quickly that they cannot be consciously perceived. When *New*

Times Magazine interviewed Tobe Hooper, producer of the film *Texas Chainsaw Massacres,* he admitted that subliminals were used to enhance the mood of the film, and went on to say that such subliminal perception can be a killer: 'The capacity of the unconscious to take information and run with it is unlimited. We flatter ourselves by thinking we are in control of our thinking.'[49] In the February 1981 edition of *Reader's Digest* Vance Packard reported one of the world's largest advertising agencies forecasting that within a few years many television messages will be coming at us in three-second blasts, combining words, symbols and other imagery.

The second category of subliminals is forward masking, in which sounds or messages are placed on to soundtracks very faintly, often on the louder parts of the recording. An early example of this has an interesting historical background. At some time in the nineteen-sixties, a rumour began to spread that Beatles superstar Paul McCartney had been killed in a road accident, and that someone else was taking his place in the group's recording sessions. It seems that the Beatles decided to foster the idea (no prizes for guessing why!) in various ways, including the use of certain album cover devices and one particular use of forward masking. On their subsequent smash hit 'Strawberry Fields Forever', one can distinctly hear a voice quietly saying, 'I buried Paul.' This was presumably no more than a distasteful stunt, but it indicates the possibilities of the device.

The third and most widespread subliminal device is backward-masking, in which words, sounds or messages are inserted backwards on to a recording. The most common use of this technique is phonetic backmasking, which allows musicians to merge song lyrics with the subliminal device. These strange sounds are inaudible on the forward cut, but when the recording is reversed one does not hear gibberish (as one might expect) but another set of spoken words which have been placed on to the recording by complex studio techniques.

The backward-masking device becomes all the more frightening when one realizes that messages inserted in this way must sometimes be demonically imposed, with demons using the singers' voices without their conscious knowledge to place phonetic backmaskings on to the recordings. These messages can then be deciphered by playing the recording backwards, even though, technically speaking, they are not present. There may be an example of this in what has been called 'one of the most beautiful and gentle songs ever written', 'Stairway to Heaven' by Robert Plant of the heavy metal band Led Zeppelin. In *Circus* magazine, Plant said, 'The song was written in fifteen minutes. Something moved my hand across the page, I think.' It has been consistently voted the most popular rock/pop song of all time (even though it is about a female junkie looking for a 'fix' of heroin). Played forwards, the song says at one point, 'The stores are all closed, but with a word she can get what she came for' (i.e. heroin); but played backwards, that part of this 'beautiful and gentle song' appears to have a very different message: 'Here's to my sweet Satan. There was a better path would make me sad – but I have Satan.'

The Crowley connection

In 1911 the famous Satanist Aleister Crowley wrote a book called *Manual on Magick*. In it, he urged his followers to gain insight into the next world (which he took to be Satan's kingdom) by doing things backwards – writing backwards, speaking backwards, walking backwards, *and playing phonograph records backwards*. The 'law of reversal' is occultic, seen in practices such as depicting upside-down crosses and reciting the Lord's Prayer backwards, and has been adopted by many rock stars who are followers of Crowley's doctrines. Crowley's picture appears on the Beatles album 'Sergeant Pepper's Lonely Hearts Club band' (top row, second from the left) while as we mentioned earlier, Jimmy Page of Led Zeppelin bought Crowley's former Scottish home and turned it into 'some kind of shrine' to the Satanist's memory.

Evidence about the amount of backward masking and other subliminal insertion that goes on is inevitably incomplete, but it would be dangerously wrong to assume that the whole idea is a scaremongering ploy invented by rock-hating fanatics. A converted rock record producer said at one stage that he knew of fifteen groups in and around the top forty in the United States who were involved in backward masking, some employing witches to insert messages worshipping Satan, others using satanic chants and seances.[50] An American radio station *Brainstorm* reported that some of the most popular albums have subliminal messages of one kind or another. Here is some of the material that has been brought to our attention.

On their album 'Back on Black', *AC/DC* have a song called 'Hell's Bells'. When played backwards, one can hear the words, 'I will mesmerize you, but he is Satan. Let me out, Satan has me prisoner.' Using the same technique, the record 'Love at first feel' has the repeated phrase: 'We serve the devil.'

On the Beatles' song 'Helter Skelter' from their 'White Album', there is the backward phrase, 'I love Satan.' It has been said that the Beatles spent 400 hours recording their smash-hit album 'Sergeant Pepper's Lonely Hearts Club Band', of which 200 hours were given to inserting subliminal material.[51] (Incidentally, this album, which became a 'classic', includes a drug-trip song 'Day in the Life' and another called 'Within you, without you', a song about Eastern mysticism.) Mass murderer Charles Manson claimed that he was motivated by 'secret voices' which he deciphered from another Beatles album 'Revolution Number Nine'.

Black Oak Arkansas have an album called 'Raunch and Roll'. In the course of the song 'When Electricity came to Arkansas', lead singer Jim Dandy makes an apparently pointless statement; but played backwards one hears the words, 'Satan, Satan, Satan. He is God, he is God, he is God.'

By slowing down the track 'You're not the one' on the 'Mirrors' LP by *Blue Oyster Cult,* the message becomes 'These women want to take advantage of my body – and furthermore our Father who art in heaven is Satan.'

Reversed messages on the album 'Hotel California' by the *Eagles* are said to include, 'Yes, Satan had help. He even organized his own religion', 'See, they're all my Satan men,' and 'I need you so, my Satan.'

On their hugely popular 'Eldorado', *Electric Light Orchestra* (popularly known as *ELO*) have a phrase which, when played backwards, runs, 'He is the nasty one, Christ, you're infernal.'

The 'Sad Wings of Destiny' album by *Judas Priest* contains the backward phrase: 'Hail Satan, send me his shining eyes.'

Led Zeppelin's 'Stairway to Heaven' is riddled with occultic philosophy. There are also satanic backward phrases, including the repeated words 'Here's to my sweet Satan.' The group's album 'Houses of the Holy' includes the song 'Over the hills and far away', which reveals the backward phrases, 'He is not forsaken. Yes, Satan is really Lord.'

When *Michael Jackson's* record 'Beat It' is played backwards, one can clearly hear the words, 'I do believe I have Satan within me.'

John Lennon and Yoko Ono released their 'Double Fantasy album a few weeks before Lennon was assassinated on 8 December 1980. By playing the song 'Kiss, Kiss, Kiss' backwards, one can hear the words, 'Satan is coming . . . 666 . . . attack, attack, attack . . . We shot John Lennon.'

Megastar *Madonna,* idolized by millions, released 'Material Girl' in 1985. It includes the backward words, 'He is the devil, Satan. I want him so, I want him so.'

When played backwards, *Motley Crue's* version of the Beatles song 'Helter Skelter' has the words, 'O Satan white, O Satan black' and 'I'm still the master.'

Subliminal words in a song by *Pink Floyd* include, 'The Lord is my shepherd. I shall not want. He maketh me to hang on hooks and high places. He converteth me to lamb cutlets. Have you heard the news? The dogs are dead' (with 'dogs' as a pseudonym for 'God').

Plasmatics' album 'Coup d'Etat' has the backward phrase, 'The brainwashed do not know they are being brainwashed.'

Prince, a high priest of sexual perversion, has a song called 'Darling Nikki' on his album 'Purple Rain'. The song is disgusting drivel about fornication and mastur-bation, but it also has a very clear reversed message: 'Hello, how are you? I'm fine, 'cos I know that the Lord is coming soon', followed by mocking laughter.

Queen's song 'Another one bites the dust' has the hidden phrase: 'Decide to smoke marijuana.'

The *Rolling Stones* have a song called 'Tops' on their 1980 album 'Tatto You'. The song is about achieving fame and fortune, and at one point it says, 'Every man is the same. Come on, I'll make you a star.' When reversed, the message becomes, 'I'm a God . . . I'm a god . . . "I love you", said the devil.'

On one of heavy metal band *Rush's* albums, 'All the World's a Stage' is the song 'Anthem', which contains the reversed confession, 'O Satan, I love you. You are the one that I need, the one that I want.'

On the *Styx* number 'Snowblind' from the album 'Paradise Theatre' there is the backward phrase, 'O Satan, move in our hearts.'

The heavy metal band *Venom* have the statement 'Satan was raised in hell' inserted into their song 'In league with Satan', while 'Welcome to hell' is the reversed greeting in the number 'At war with Satan'.

Occult international

Subliminal insertion is by no means confined to the English and American rock scenes. On a visit to Brazil Peter Anderson discovered that the overlaying of demonic and satanic suggestions was common among the records of many top recording stars in that country. Robert Carlos is one of Brazil's leading artists, with many best-selling records to his name. On his album 'Revelation' there are the reversed words, 'Satan for me. You are a star. You are the one who has helped me most.'

Jesse is another Brazilian superstar: yet she has recorded material on which the reversed words, 'Satan, devil, king, lord, you have brought me to you . . .use me' can be discerned. Magic Balloon is a highly popular group, yet one of its songs veils the chilling statement: 'Throw in the net and take out those that are high on Jesus.' Luiz Miguel's material includes the masked message: 'Satan wants peace, but Christ wants to divide this peace . . . Satan . . . Satan.' Alecew Valencia has a best-selling record which includes the hidden phrase, 'Jehovah is dirty, bow down to the devil.' Then there is Xuxu, a very popular artiste sponsored by the legendary soccer star Pele and who runs a highly rated children's programme on Brazilian TV nearly every day of the week. Backward messages found on her records include the statement, 'Satan is working, Satan lives, Satan is life.'

It is obviously impossible to get a world-wide picture of the subliminal phenomenon, or to quantify its effect, but we recently had a simple illustration of the fact that this kind of material does 'get through'. A young Christian told us that he got a strange feeling when listening to the top-selling Michael Jackson LP 'The Thriller Album'. Before he could say anything further, we told him that the track that was causing him problems was called 'Beat it'. 'You're absolutely right', he replied, 'but how did you know?' Our answer was to tell him that that was the only track on the album alleged to contain satanic backward masking.

Christ and Belial?

There is no telling how many other countries have their musical media infiltrated in this way, but one could be forgiven for supposing that at least this is confined to secular music; yet there seems to be evidence that this is not the case – and in two different areas. In some instances, there seems to have been an attempt to use the backward masking device to get a Christian message across, and we have been given several illustrations of this. In these cases, the motives may be commendable, but one has to question the wisdom and morality of using subliminal techniques in communicating biblical truth. What about Paul's statement to the Corinthians that the wisdom he speaks is 'not the wisdom of this age or of the rulers of this age, who are coming to nothing' (1 Corinthians 2:6), or his later statement that 'The weapons we fight with are not the weapons of the world. On the contrary, they have divine power to demolish strongholds'? (2 Corinthians 10:4).

The other, almost unbelievable area is that in which there is evidence of blasphemous and downright satanic material subliminally inserted into recordings made by Christian singers and musicians. We are not suggesting that this is done with the knowledge or consent of the Christian performers concerned, but in view of the large number of people involved between the writing of a song and the sale of a record, the situation calls for the strictest possible monitoring at every stage of production.

Stryper

There does not appear to have been backward masking in the case of Stryper, a 'Christian' heavy metal band hugely popular on both sides of the Atlantic. But there are sinister signs behind the headlines. In the United States Stryper record on the Enigma label. Yet all Enigma's record covers have a small 'satanic blessing' symbol on the back, consisting of a crescent with a small black blob placed under a rather 'wobbly' pyramid (pyramid power is a common occultic feature). *This satanic symbol appears on Stryper's LP's,* including those imported into the UK and distributed by Word (UK) Ltd. The cover of their LP 'To Hell with the Devil' also has an occultic pentagram (a five-pointed star in a circle). When Peter Anderson showed a Stryper record cover to a Brazilian evangelist, converted from an occultic background, he immediately recognized the symbol as one used in *macumba,* the Brazilian equivalent of voodoo.

It is admittedly difficult to see how this can find its way into the music, yet when a German missionary played a Stryper record to a group of Indians in the Amazonian rain forest, the natives told him that it was 'good spirit music' – and their meaning was obvious.

What do others make of Stryper? Douglas Kennedy begins an article in *The Listener* like this: 'At first sight they look like your typical exponents of five-car-pile-up rock music. With their studded leather pants, fitting like surgical gloves, their heavily permed, shoulder-length hair and their silver neck halters, the four California boys who make up the group called Stryper seem to be either bondage fetishists or bikers with bizarre Nazi tendencies. And when they appear on stage, in front of an adoring public' (later said by Kennedy to be mainly 'middle-aged women and their pubescent daughters'), 'they indulge in all the usual mannerisms and theatrical pyrotechnics associated with heavy metal music – Armageddon lighting effects, explosions, a lot of sweaty gymnastics.'[52] Kennedy did not mention their faces which were daubed with lipstick and mascara, nor the black and yellow spandex tights, and gave no assessment of what even one of their sympathetic critics has described as their 'ear-smashing music'.[53] However far removed we may find these things to be from a godly presentation of the gospel (and we have to say that we find them repugnant) we are nevertheless not suggesting that any member of the group is personally and deliberately involved in occultism or anything like it. We will assume that these men are genuinely concerned to serve God through the medium of heavy metal music. But in the light of the Bible's clear commands for Christians to separate themselves from the works of darkness, it is difficult to see why the group remains linked with a company that actively promotes satanic heavy metal and insists on putting occultic symbols on its record sleeves. Enigma holds no brief for the gospel; surely Stryper's contract is not worth more to the group than maintaining biblical principles?

What are we to make of all this? What proportion of the vast pop music output is affected? What hard evidence is there that the messages get through? To be fair, these must in part remain open questions. Wild exaggeration would obviously be foolish – but so would a casual 'there's nothing in it' attitude. Satan is not called 'the god of this age' (2 Corinthians 4:4) for nothing, and to limit his power and subtlety to what we think is either possible or likely is to play right into his hands. Hysteria may not be the right response to the subliminal issue – but neither is apathy.

Under the influence

Many of the quotations in this chapter refer to the personal beliefs and feelings of rock performers. Here are some other statements that speak even more directly to the question of whether the music of those concerned is directly under the influence of occultic powers. Frank Zappa once boasted, 'I am the devil's advocate.'[54] Jim Steinman, song writer for Meat Loaf, once said, 'I have always been fascinated by the supernatural and always felt rock was *the perfect idiom* for it.'[55] Singer David Bowie admits, 'Rock 'n' roll will destroy you. It lets in lower elements and shadows. *Rock has always been the devil's music.*'[56] Mick Jones of The Clash adds, 'There's definitely some inner magic circle with rock 'n' roll. We've encountered it enough times to be certain of that.'[57] These statements, coming from the heart of the modern rock scene, are very explicit. But perhaps even more significant is this comment from Bob Larson, rock singer turned evangelist, from whose works we have already quoted: 'As a minister I know now what it is like to feel the unction of the Holy Spirit. As a rock musician, I knew what it meant to feel the counterfeit anointing of Satan.'[58] What makes Larson's statement so significant is that unlike many musicians we have examined, he was never 'into' the occult world. He speaks of the 'anointing of Satan' not in the context of his interest in the occult (which was non-existent) but in the context of his immersion in rock music. Is there nothing to be learned from that?

Of course, there are those involved in the production and marketing of 'Christian' rock music who will suggest that this smacks of a 'holier-than-thou' witch-hunt and that secular observers don't see things that way. But that is not the case. Even as this book was on its way to the publisher, *Time* ran a feature on Jerry Lee Lewis, a major rock 'n' roll star in the early nineteen-sixties, who had just released a 209-song collection on twelve albums to celebrate his years at the top of the tree. After documenting Lewis's problems with alcohol, drugs, miscellaneous creditors and several ex-wives, *Time* reporter

Jay Cocks quotes Lewis as saying, 'You've got to walk and talk with God to go to heaven . . . I have the devil in me![59] The report then ends with this comment: 'Indeed, periodically seized by remorse over a misspent life, Lewis will still ruminate over making a stand for God. But the devil – the music, and the life that goes with it – always wins out. Shared or not, that fundamental faith gives Jerry Lee's music, even to a heathen, the unique power of sin. No smart talk or side-stepping for him. This is the devil's music, and Jerry Lee Lewis plays it with the aplomb of a peer. He may smell damnation himself, but that unholy gift of his has surely secured him a place in rock 'n' roll's heaven. Right up there in the dark. At the end of the road.'[60]

But musicians under satanic influence will almost inevitably result in listeners coming under the same influence. Bob Larson says elsewhere, 'It is possible that any person who has danced for substantial lengths of time to rock music may have come under the oppressive, obsessive or possessive influence of demons.'[61] For 'danced' read 'listened', and you have the potential for even greater physical, mental, spiritual and moral disaster.

Let us give just one illustration of what we mean. We have personal knowledge of a girl in whose room solid objects were moved around by an unseen force. Looking into the dressing table mirror, she saw frightening apparitions. The atmosphere in the room was so terrifying that even her pet dog would not enter it. Pinned to the inside of the door to her room was the sleeve of a rock record by the group 999, but it had been placed on the door upside down, so that it read '666'. In the absence of other known factors, it was assumed that this was the connection with the abnormal happenings in the room. As soon as the record sleeve was taken down and destroyed, the atmosphere in the room returned to normal, the apparitions ceased – and even the dog came happily back into the room.

This is just one small glimpse of the frightening power that can be unleashed even through seemingly innocuous objects connected with the occult. Yet *Buzz* can calmly assure its readers that 'To teach that to be in the same room as a Led Zeppelin record is to leave oneself open to demon possession is unscriptural nonsense'![62]

Put out that fire!

We entitled this chapter 'Strange fire'. The phrase comes from the Old Testament, where we read that Aaron's sons Nadab and Abihu 'offered *strange fire* before the Lord, which the Lord had not commanded them' (Leviticus 10:1 NASB). The meaning of the words is not given, but in the New International Version they are translated 'unauthorized fire', and that helps us to get a clearer picture. God had given very specific instructions about the preparation and offering of sacrifices. Certain things were taboo; precise rules had to govern what they did. But Nadab and Abihu ignored God's commands and 'did their own thing'. The result was disastrous; we read that moments later 'fire came out from the presence of the Lord and consumed them, and they died before the Lord' (Leviticus 10:2).

The severity of the punishment shows the seriousness of their sin – and is a clear warning to us today, not least in this area of rock music. But along with the warning the Bible gives us an equally clear command: 'For you were once darkness, but now you are light in the Lord. Live as children of light (for the fruit of the light consists in all goodness, righteousness and truth) and find out what pleases the Lord. Have nothing to do with the fruitless deeds of darkness, but rather expose them' (Ephesians 5:8-11).

Putting the negative warning and the positive command together, our message to the Christian rock music fan is clear and simple: *put out the fire*! Demonstrate once and for all your allegiance to Christ and your opposition to Satan by clearing these musicians' material out of your life and out of your home – records, tapes, books, magazines, posters, clothing, badges – *everything*. God certainly intends you to have music in your life but 'What harmony is there between Christ and Belial?' (2 Corinthians 6:15).

Dave Roberts adds this good advice: 'If you are serious about being a disciple of Christ you should not lay yourself open to possible demonic influence through these records. You should destroy them and discontinue buying material of that nature. Do not trot out pathetic excuses about not listening to the words either. If you don't think about what you are listening to then you will find your subconscious mind is slowly poisoned by these celebrations of lust and the occult.'[63] This last comment ties in exactly with the warning given by Bob Larson: 'Whether or not a person listening to an occult-rock song is consciously listening to the words really makes no difference. The subconscious mind, the seat of the soul, is being affected.'[64]

What about material from other performers? You could certainly begin by checking the words, the sounds and the album covers. Closer examination might tell you a lot more than you realized. And if in doubt, *never give the benefit of that doubt to the devil!* To encourage you, here is an extract from a letter we received from a young couple, youth leaders in their local church, after reading the first edition of *Pop Goes the Gospel:* 'After reading through your book, we looked through our record collection and had to decide that at least £300 worth needed to be destroyed. At first we did not want to destroy the records. £300 is a lot of money and we were both unemployed. Then we thought, "Why not sell them?" – but we soon put paid to that. Of course it is no use selling such blatant anti-Christian rubbish; it needs to be destroyed, and we know (and actually knew right from the start) that that was the only action to take. It was like getting the victory over a bad habit; it is difficult (or seems to be) at the beginning, but if you really want to get rid of it, then the Lord can help you and it is not too difficult at all. If you really love the Lord, then destroying a few records like that becomes a real pleasure.'

Of course throwing out occultic or doubtful material will not be an automatic passport to holiness. The Bible has a story in Matthew 12 about an evil spirit leaving a man but returning later to repossess him with seven spirits worse than itself, because although the man's house was swept clean it was 'unoccupied' (Matthew 12:44). Make sure that evil is replaced by good. That could mean better music – music that is glorifying to God. It might also mean using your time more productively than in passively soaking up godless philosophies and values!

5.
Danger signals

In the last two chapters we have looked at the more sinister elements associated with rock music, though it could be argued that these flow into the music rather than out of it. Nobody seriously suggests that sexual aberration or occultism are *parts* of the music. Having said that, the connection is clear and close and there is no doubt that rock music is a powerful communicator of their damaging philosophies.

But that is by no means the end of the story. Rock music must by now have been blamed for almost every evil under the sun, from atheism to the crime rate. We suspect that someone, somewhere might be on the verge of blaming it for bad weather or crop failure! Perhaps it is not too surprising that rock gets a lot of 'flak', and not only from people who have never been a part of it. Jerry Lee Lewis, one of the founders of the rock 'n' roll subculture, was later reported as saying, 'I am sorry that I was involved in the beginnings of rock and roll. I never dreamed it would take the course it has taken. It has helped to destroy untold millions of young people the world over.'[1] Other than those we have already mentioned, what other areas are part of the rock music scene?

Pills and needles

Drug abuse is an obvious example. Much of this can be

traced to the rise of the hippie movement in the nineteen-sixties. Many of the pop songs which became all the
rage then encouraged young people to get turned on to
drugs, while others included drug-related lyrics without
comment – and the lead came from the top. The Beatles'
record-breaking album 'Sergeant Pepper's Lonely
Hearts Club Band' was described by *Time* magazine as
'drenched in drugs'.[2]

One of the songs on the album, 'Magical Mystery
Tour', invited the listeners, 'Roll up your sleeve, roll up
your sleeve, the magical mystery tour is coming to take
you away.' In 'Rainy Day Woman', Bob Dylan advo-
cated 'getting stoned', while his song 'Mr Tambourine
Man' has been called 'the best of the drugs songs'.[3] By
the end of the decade the Le Dain Commission
appointed by the Canadian government to study the
drug problem, reported, 'The pop music industry has
played a major role in encouraging drug use in general
and marijuana in particular.'[4] Addressing the second
Annual International Music Conference, Paul G. Marshall, spokesman for a major record industry advertising
company, said, 'Record companies and music publishers
have earned many millions of dollars from records extol-
ling the virtues of drugs.'

During the Vietnam War, the United States Government wanted to send a top rock group to entertain the
troops, but had possible groups screened first to ensure
that they were clear of drugs. The plan had to be abandoned because a 'clean' group could not be found.

In 1969 *Time* magazine said, 'Rock musicians use
drugs frequently and openly, and their compositions are
riddled with references to drugs, from the Beatles' "I get
High With A Little Bit Of Help From My Friends" to
Jefferson Airplane's "White Rabbit".'[5]

Not much seems to have changed. In 1979 a leading
rock group manager stated, 'No matter what anyone

tells you, drugs will always be a part of the rock scene,'[6] while in the same magazine rock critic Robert Forbes added, 'Drugs are a necessary ingredient for many rock musicians.'[7] The Rolling Stones are among a number of groups still pushing drug songs, with 'Brown Sugar' (S.E.Asian cocaine), 'Sweet Sister Morphine' and 'Cousin Cocaine' as examples. Among those openly admitting to taking drugs are Mick Jagger, The Bee Gees, Jerry Garcia, the Doobie Brothers, Glenn Frey, Linda Rondstadt and Gregg Allman; how many others do is anybody's guess. There is a tragic list of those who have died as the result of drugs, with Jimi Hendrix, Janis Joplin, Jim Morrison, Al Wilson (Canned Heat), Gram Parsons and Gary Thain (Uriah Heep), Vinnie Taylor (Sha Na Na), Keith Moon (the Who), Tommy Bolin (Deep Purple), Robbie McIntosh (Average White Band), Sid Vicious (Sex Pistols) and Lowell George (Little Feat) among them.

By March 1983 Customs and Excise officials in Britain reported that heroin seized by them in the previous twelve months had a street value of £59,000,000 (an increase of 178% over the previous year's figure) and that drugs of various kinds were being smuggled into Britain at a street value rate of £1,500,000 *per day*. Not surprisingly, one university student told us that drugs were 'as easy to get as coffee'. How drugs and music merge is unclear, but there are alarming stories of the result. Jean Alison told *Reader's Digest* the story of her son's LSD trips being set off again by 'one of the tunes he had been singing'.[8] Even more alarmingly, *Young Life* reported that a young man, converted to Christ ten years previously and miraculously healed of hard drug addiction, went to Greenbelt and started hallucinating for the first time since he became a Christian as soon as he got there![9] Can we just dismiss that out of hand? What we can be sure about is that anything that might help to create that kind of syndrome should be avoided like the plague.

Give a dog a bad name

Other elements have helped to give rock a bad name, too. *Violence* is one of these and not just when Alice Cooper splits open live chickens and throws their intestines over the audience. Groups like the Cream produced 'a sort of subliminal violence with which their audience could involve themselves'.[10] Ted Nugent, who calls his music 'combat rock' (and wears earplugs while performing it), speaks of raping his audience.[11] Mick Jagger of the Rolling Stones is reported as saying, 'Ours is a group with built-in hate. We communicate aggression and frustration to an audience, musically and visually.' A group called Napalm Death, and claiming to be the fastest thrash band in the world, released an album called 'From Enslavement to Obliteration'. Reviewing a record by Festering Pus, one writer said, 'It is bilious, bullying and blooming brutal.'[12] Allen Lanier of Blue Oyster Cult, admitted that 'Rock and roll brings out violent emotions. There's a lot of violence, a lot of aggression in the music.'[13]

It is just as disturbing to find this element of violence in so-called Christian records. In 1988 MTV rejected a pop video by the Christian heavy metal group DeGarmo and Key on the grounds that it was excessively violent![14]

There is a mindless brutality about heavy metal and the like and no Christian should have anything to do with it.

Rebellion has been another of rock's companions. Warning that most adults are only concerned about the *noise* of heavy metal music, *Newsweek* said, 'It's not just the earsplitting sound and the relentless beat. Kids at a heavy metal concert don't sit in their seats; they stand on them and move – it's the spirit of rebellion.'[15] David Lee Roth of the group Van Halen told *USA Today*, 'We like the fact that the masses see us as rock 'n' roll rebels.'[16] Even Elvis Costello, whose image is somewhat docile at times, says, 'The only two things that motivate me and that matter to me are revenge and guilt. They are the only emotions I know about. Love? I don't know what it means. It doesn't exist in my songs.'[17] George Melly even suggests that 'A pop movement is attractive precisely because it proposed a revolt.'[18]

Speaking on a BBC Radio 4 programme *Crooning Buffoons,* Ray Gosling went even further: 'Rock 'n' roll is a beast. Well-intentioned people thought you could pick it up and cuddle it. They forgot it had claws . . . Next time you pass a record shop window . . . look at the names of the bands – The Slits, The Damned, Bad Manners, The Vibrators, The Stranglers and Meat Loaf. The march of the Mods in 1964 was no twentieth-century version of the Durham Miners' Gala. It was sawdust Caesars putting the boot in . . . nasty as a boil, every one of them. I know, because I was one of them. Behind every sweet doowop and bebop is an unfettered sexuality and sympathy for the devil: a violently anarchic — in the face of all harmony, peace and progress. People could see that when it first happened and it hasn't changed. Anybody with a penn'orth of grey matter could see it was trouble.'[19]

No doubt he had a wider perspective in mind, but it is worth quoting these words by Alexander Solzhenitsyn when he gave the Harvard University Graduation Address in 1978, in which he expressed his reasons for the West's decline: 'The human soul longs for things higher, warmer and purer that those offered by today's intolerable music.'

The Bible's teaching is that 'Everyone must submit

himself to the governing authorities, for there is no authority except that which God has established. The authorities that exist have been established by God. Consequently, he who rebels against the authority is rebelling against what God has instituted, and those who do so will bring judgement on themselves' (Romans 13:1-2). Incidentally, this points indirectly to the dangers of the popular fad of speaking about a 'Jesus revolution'. Rather than thinking in terms of any kind of revolt, Christians should concentrate on their responsibility to be 'blameless and pure, children of God without fault in a crooked and depraved generation' (Philippians 2:15).

In God's name

Another element in rock music is widespread *blasphemy*. As long ago as 1964 the Beatles' press officer Derek Taylor said, 'It's as if they'd founded a new religion. They're completely anti-Christ. I mean I'm anti-Christ as well, but they're so anti-Christ they shock me, which is not an easy thing.'[20] John Lennon once referred to Christ as a 'garlic eating, stinking, little yellow greasy fascist bastard Catholic Spaniard'.[21] David Bowie sank even lower and once stated, 'Jesus Christ was a strange boy himself.'[22] Others are equally blasphemous and anti-Christian in their beliefs, their behaviour and their music, but have found ways of expressing their philosophies more subtly. John Lennon made this clear shortly before he died: 'Rock music has got the same message as before. It is anti-religious, anti-nationalistic and anti-morality. But now I understand what you have to do. You have to put the message across with a little honey on it.' But can the two go together? Little

Richard, one of the founders of the rock 'n' roll era, knows the answer to that one: 'Rock 'n' roll doesn't glorify God. You can't drink out of God's cup and the devil's cup at the same time. I was one of the pioneers of that music, one of the builders. I know what the blocks are made of, because I built them.'[23]

Blasphemy became the state of the art with the two hugely popular musicals *Godspell* and *Jesus Christ Superstar*. The script of *Godspell* is partly paraphrased from the words of Matthew's Gospel, and was hailed by many Christians as an exciting breakthrough in communicating the gospel to the masses – a marvellous way to get the name of Jesus out to millions of people who would seldom if ever darken the doors of a church. Even the now defunct Christian magazine *Crusade* wrote approvingly of it. But the musical's author Stephen Schwartz said, 'I wrote it because Christianity is the biggest myth there is around and I'm going to show what a myth it is by making a joke out of it.' One of the ways in which Schwartz did this was by dressing the characters as clowns and then having them parody Scripture, such as when John the Baptist baptized Jesus with a sponge, making sure to clean behind the ears.

Jesus Christ Superstar, which became the biggest money-making musical in history, also received an enthusiastic reception from many Christians – yet it was financed by Robert Stigwood, a homosexual rock promoter, and written by Timothy Rice and Andrew Lloyd Webber, both of whom admitted to being atheists at the time. Interviewed on an American radio station, Rice said, 'Basically, the idea of the whole opera is to have Christ seen through the eyes of Judas, Christ as man and not as God, and the fact that Christ himself is just as mixed up and unaware of what he is as Judas is.' On another occasion he said, 'It happens that we don't see

Christ as God, but simply the right man at the right time in the right place.'[24] Those are very significant statements. They show that Bible words were being used, *but were conveying something less than biblical truth*. The tragedy is that multitudes of Christians fell for it. The secular press was not always so gullible, with the film critic of *Newsweek* making this comment on the film version: 'It is one of the two fiascos of modern cinema. It has fatal foolishness everywhere . . . We danced and sang and Jesus was crucified and a good time was had by all. Lord, forgive them. They know not what they are doing.'[25] Yet the very fact that these two musicals were generally so popular among non-Christians should have warned believers of their dangers. As Bob Larson says, 'Any time the world begins to sing about Jesus, Christians should beware . . . The world hates Christ as much as it did when the multitudes crucified him.'[26]

The two superhits are now part of modern musical folklore, yet in some measure they paved the way for a situation now so bad that Graham Cray can say of rock music in general that '*Most of it* is used as a vehicle for anti-Christian propaganda.'[27] The Christian's response should be obvious. No amount of liking the music gives him warrant to surround himself with music whose philosophies and values are in blasphemous opposition to the one who alone is 'King of kings and Lord of lords' (Revelation 19:16).

Body blows

There are further danger signals when we turn to take a closer look at some of the potential effects of rock music on the lives of those who listen to it and the first of these warns us that rock music can be *physically damaging*. We touched on this in an earlier chapter when we looked at loud amplification as one of the essential elements in rock – and we can take our cue from there. Articles in the secular press continue to make the point: writing in the *Leicester Mercury* under the headline 'Will the sound of music drive us mad?' Charles Fraser said, 'Irate parents have suspected it for years and now medical authorities are coming to the same conclusion . . . deafening rock music can drive you mad.'[28] A leading educationalist Dr D. M. Beaumont asks, 'Why have music that can lead to hysteria and in the long term to schizophrenia?'[29] At an international conference on noise pollution, a World Health Authority expert testified that loud rock music could cause deafness, psychiatric problems and even temporary insanity.[30]

There is certainly no questioning the physical assault mounted by some forms of rock, such as heavy metal. As Bob Larson says, 'Rock, at least in its harsher forms, doesn't tickle your ears. It jams you in the skull like a freight train. You don't *listen* to loud rock; it baptizes you with a liturgy of sex, drugs, perversion and the occult.'[31] *Buzz* columnist Dave Roberts agrees: 'Heavy rock is body music designed to bypass your brain and with an unrelenting brutality induce a frenzied state amongst the audience.'[32] In the same article he says that heavy metal, punk and disco attempt to dominate and master the hearer.[33]

That last point is important. For many performers the avalanche of decibels is a deliberate and important part of their total intention. It is *meant* to blast the emotions and the mind – not to reflect truth, honesty, integrity or beauty, nor to encourage a discerning response or produce any beneficial result. When David Porter says of rock music that 'It is primarily a physical thing,'[34] he hits the nail on the head. So does Mick Farren when he says, 'Rock music is not something you understand, it is something you feel with your body and you know.'[35] In an

article in *Reader's Digest* entitled 'We're poisoning ourselves with sound', James Stewart Gordon detailed
some of the serious effects of noise on the human body.
One of his conclusions was that 'Noise is most damaging
when it is loud, meaningless, irregular and unpredict-
able'[36] – an unintentional but accurate description of a
great deal of today's rock music. There are hidden dangers, too. Equipment used by today's rock groups deliv-
ers sound at both infrasonic and ultrasonic levels (below
and above the hearing range) and scientists are becoming increasingly disturbed by the potential threat to
health that this poses.[37]

Down-to-earth evidence for the negative effects of
rock music has come from many sources. In *Times on
Sunday,* correspondent Martin Walker reported from
Moscow that Soviet researchers found that heavy metal
music caused physical damage. The research project,
described in *Sovyetskaya Rossiya* as 'a stunning discov-
ery' claimed that 'The wilder the music, the lower is the
level of young people's working ability.' Professor G.
Aminev, Head of the Psychology Department at
Bashkiria University, claimed that 'Heavy metal listeners are affected by the psycho-physiological mechanisms
of addiction. If they are isolated from such music for a
week their general level of health declines, they become
more irritable, their hands start to tremble and their
pulse becomes irregular. Some of them refused to continue with our experiments after the third day. This
means we are witnessing a certain kind of illness. It
seems that rock music does not only have a psychological
influence but a biochemical one too, for it seems connected with the appearance of the morphine type sub-
stances which induce "pleasure".' Professor Aminev
went on to say that studies of Soviet schoolchildren after
they had been to heavy metal discos showed 'a worsen-
ing of memory, loss of attention, a fall in reading speeds

and an increase in aggressiveness and stubbornness'.[38]

The sounds of music

There are even other less obvious dangers associated with certain sounds. Timothy Leary, the psychologist who began the nineteen-sixties as a Harvard professor and ended the decade as a drop-out serving a Californian jail sentence for the possession of marijuana, claimed evidence that music of a certain kind had effects similar to those produced by toxic drugs. Adrenalin secretions generated by over-stimulated glands led, he claimed, to imbalanced and harmful physical reactions. More recently, others have confirmed this. David Noebel says, 'Under rock music, the secretion of hormones is more pronounced . . . which causes an abnormal imbalance in the body's system, lowers the blood sugar and calcium levels and impairs judgement.'[39] Noebel also cites medical evidence that 'The low frequency vibrations of the bass guitar, along with the driving beat of the drum, affect the cerebrospinal fluid, which in turn affects the pituitary gland, which in turn directs the secretions of hormones in the body.'[40] Even more remarkable is this statement by Cyril Scott: 'Our researches have proved to us that not only the emotional content but *the essence of the actual musical form* tends to reproduce itself in human conduct.'[41]

We are not left guessing as to the kind of 'human conduct' to which hard rock can lead. The *Daily Mirror* reports that 'A night out at a rock concert ended in tragedy for schoolboy Chris Tyrer. He died after joining in a "head banging" session. It is the dance in which youngsters shake their heads from side to side in time to the music. Chris was seen "head banging" as 1,000 fans watched the rock group Saxon at Wolverhampton Civic

Hall. The next morning his parents found him paralysed down one side. He died in hospital eight days later.'[42] Even more horrendous is the story of Mark Silman. The teenager from Tilehurst, Reading, a former Elvis Presley fanatic, killed a fifteen-year-old girl by stabbing her eighty-five times with a ten-inch butcher's knife. The *Reading Chronicle* reported that he had modelled himself on a rock singer with the group the Meteors, who sing about blood and violence and drink blood on stage.[43]

These cases may be extreme, but they are certainly not unique – and we can assume that there are countless other young people who are being physically damaged because of exposure to the kind of sound rock singer Ted Nugent had in mind when he said, 'Rock is the perfect primal method of releasing our violent instincts.'[44]

This leads to the obvious question: has any Christian, whose body is 'a temple of the Holy Spirit' (1 Corinthians 6:19), the right, for the selfish satisfaction of his own musical tastes, to expose himself for even one moment to the kind of music that can potentially lead to such consequences?

It's all in the mind

Not only can rock music be physically damaging, another area of danger is that it opens the door to *psychological manipulation*. Dr William Shafer is quite blunt about it: 'Rock music is a tool for altering consciousness.'[45] So is Robert Palmer of the *New York Times,* who claimed that using music to induce altered states of consciousness had become one of the most significant musical trends of the nineteen-eighties and that rock musicians were beginning to explore the possibilities of rhythmic and modal repetition, which seeks through absolute control of limited musical means to induce certain psychological states. In their book *Super Learning*, Sheila Ostrander and Lynn Schroeder write, 'The idea that music can affect your body and your mind certainly isn't new . . . For centuries, from Asia to the Middle East to South America people have used music to carry them into unusual states of consciousness. The key has always been to find just the right kind of music for just the right kind of effect.'[46]

The Communist regimes have made intensive studies into ways of conditioning people. One Bulgarian doctor, after fifteen years' research on the use of music in conditioning says, 'Certain drumbeats act as a kind of pacemaker, regulating brain-wave rhythms and breathing, which leads to biochemical changes that produce altered states of consciousness. If you listen to a different drummer, you do see a different world.'[47] In a remarkable book called *The Science of Yoga*, I. K. Taimni comes to the same conclusion: 'There is a fundamental relationship between vibration and consciousness, because each level of consciousness has a specific vibration associated with it.'[48] In his book *Subliminal Seduction*, Dr Wilson Bryan Key tells of advertising companies spending fortunes researching how music can be used to influence people. Some discovered that a seventy-two-beats-a-minute rhythm increases suggestibility and that a television commercial with such a beat produced the headache symptoms that the product being advertised was supposed to cure.[49]

But the evidence for psychological manipulation does not come from outside sources alone. Rock musicians have been saying the same thing for a long time, though in simpler, cruder ways. Timothy Leary was certainly on to it: his song 'Turn on, tune in, drop out' became an anthem for millions, and Leary's comment on it was 'Don't listen to the words, it's the music that has its own

message . . . I've been stoned on the music many times
. . . The music is what will get you going.'[50] Graham Nash
said, 'Pop music is *the* mass medium for conditioning the
way people think.'[51] Pop singer Donovan agreed: 'Rock
music is the music for affecting consciousness.' Drummer Spencer Dryden was quite clear how this power
should be used: 'Get them when they're young. Bend
the minds.'[52] Mick Jagger said much the same thing:
'We're moving after the minds and so are most of the
new groups.'[53] In *Melody Maker* he said, 'Communication is the answer to the whole of the world's problems
and music is the key to it all because music opens the
door to everybody's mind.'[54]

High or deep?

Of course it is not only rock music that can be used in
psychological manipulation. The same can be true of
classical music. Hitler used some of Wagner's music to
crank up the crowds – and even parts of Handel's *Messiah* when he wanted to create a pseudo-religious atmosphere. Even the best of music can be used from the worst
of motives.

One secret of music's great power is that it appeals so
directly to the subconscious. As a result, people soak up
the meaning of music without being aware that they are
doing so. Add to that the volume level, constant repetition and incessant beat which are so much a part of rock
music, and the scene is set for the conditioning process.
As Cedric Cullingford wrote in *The Guardian,* 'Far from
being a palpable alternative culture with its own clear
ideas, pop music is something absorbed at a subconscious level.'[55] Many young Christians have told us that
they feel perfectly safe in listening to records containing
perverted lyrics because 'We don't listen to the words,

we just happen to like the music.' But they have missed the vital point that the music *itself* is affecting them at an even deeper level *without their knowing it*.

Surely the dangers of all this are obvious – and not least in communicating the gospel. Evangelists have sometimes been told during a lively gospel concert, 'Don't worry, we'll bring them down before you speak.' But why do the listeners need to be 'brought down' before hearing the gospel? What were they 'up' on? An emotional 'high'? Then why were they taken up there? Presumably as a preliminary to the preaching! The whole thing becomes a tragic nonsense. Why is it important to get a crowd 'high'? That kind of conditioning amounts to trying to do the work of the Holy Spirit for him. There is certainly a right kind of preparation for the hearing of God's Word, but excessive volume, driving beat, repetitious phrases and the like are not the biblical way to go about it. Musical conditioning is not the same as the Holy Spirit challenging the mind to think, the spirit to be still and the heart to be humbled in the presence of God.

In closing this chapter, let us ask a very important question. In loading our evangelistic programmes with manipulative music, are we not greatly increasing the risk of producing 'conversions' that are psychological rather than spiritual? The set-up could not be more perfect. Impressionable young people can undoubtedly be so conditioned by the music that they are much more likely to accept whatever the preacher says. Add a good communicator and the chances are that he will produce an impressive number of 'decisions'. However, the danger is that these 'decisions' are the result of musical conditioning rather than spiritual conviction. We will take a closer look at this in the next chapter. 'But evangelists can be manipulators too,' somebody says, 'even those who do not use a great deal of music.' Yes they can – and when they are, the eventual results are just as disappointing. It would not be difficult to prove that the best 'manipulators' among evangelists are among those who produce the most impressive immediate statistics – *but the numbers that count are those that continue*.

Everybody enjoys music of one kind or another. Add its power to stir the emotions of its listeners, recognize the fact that rock music in particular is such a tremendous attraction to young people, and the idea of using it in the work of evangelism seems obvious and natural. But evangelism is not about the natural; it is about the spiritual. We are serving a God who says, 'My thoughts are not your thoughts, neither are your ways my ways' (Isaiah 55:8) and in evangelism, as in every other area of life, the all-important thing is not to go along with the majority, not even the Christian majority, but to 'find out what pleases *the Lord*' (Ephesians 5:10).

6.
Pop goes the gospel

If 'Christian music' does not actually exist, nobody
seems to have told today's church! Within the last
hundred years a thriving tradition of music has taken
root in its evangelistic programme. The most popular
movement in Britain was fired to a large extent by the
work of Ira D. Sankey, civil servant turned gospel musician, who accompanied the great American evangelist
D. L. Moody to this country on his evangelistic campaigns in 1873. Five years later William Booth founded
the Salvation Army and wrote, 'Every note, every
strain, and every harmony is divine and belongs to us . . .
bring out your cornets and harps and organs and flutes
and violins and pianos and drums, and everything else
that can make a melody. Offer them to God, and use
them to make all the hearts about you merry before the
Lord.'[1] The reverberations were loud and long, but the
real explosion was to come eighty years later.

Rock hits the road

As we saw earlier, rock 'n' roll arrived on the scene in the
early nineteen-fifties. Very soon, it swept around the
Western world, and before long Christians were beginning to see it as a potential vehicle for the gospel. Today,
the emphasis on pop music in British evangelism,

especially among young people, is almost overpowering, with advertisements for musical events, 'happenings', celebrations, festivals, concerts and 'gigs' cramming the pages of the popular Christian youth press.

The religious road show has become a major feature, with an apparently endless succession of musical tours around the country. At one point we found current notices for over 500 musical events. Not that they have been unanimously welcomed – many ministers pressurized into encouraging their churches' support have come away disillusioned. Bill Spencer, editor of *Evangelism Today,* wrote, 'As tour after tour drags our young people away from reality the time has surely come for people to make their objections known. Is it too much to hope that the young will somewhere be able to hear a word from God without the use of banks of loudspeakers and flashing lights?'[2]

Then there are the 'static' events: the Greenbelt rock festival attracts over 25,000 people and several other more 'traditional' gatherings are leaning in the same direction. Alongside the tours and the larger set pieces a whole industry has sprung up, kept solvent by thousands of young Christians who cheerfully keep the cash flowing in for records, tapes, tickets, posters, stickers, T-shirts and other associated paraphernalia.

Question time

But in the absence of biblical examples for this kind of evangelism it is surely important to ask some questions. What motivates the musicians? What prompts the promoters? Are we to imagine that they are all devil-inspired 'moles', infiltrating the Christian church in order to destroy it from the inside? Of course not –

though it goes without saying that in an industry of this size there are bound to be rogues of one kind or another. Not all of those involved in hyping the teenage market do so from purely spiritual motives. Dennis Disney, Nashville marketing director of World Records ('the biggest Christian communications company in the world') says quite openly, 'We actively seek out rockers who are ministry-orientated, but with a strong sales potential – a Christian artist *who can bring a return on our investment.*'[3] The emphasis is ours – and his! No wonder Douglas Kennedy can tell readers of *The Listener* that 'Christian music has gone commercial with a vengeance.'[4] Some of the performers would not even claim to be Christians. Tom Morton, at the time a full-time musician with British Youth for Christ, wrote quite openly about this: 'What has happened over the last fifteen years in Britain has been the formation of a Christian music "scene", featuring record companies, management agencies, tour organizers, full-time performers, concert promoters and assorted hangers-on. Instead of this subculture being rooted in Christian standards in fact as well as in name, it appears that some of the Christian music scene has become, in effect, sub-Christian. Some Christian musicians seem excessively concerned with fame, with their image; some record companies seem profit-orientated at the expense of their artists' ministries, and since their "package" is wrapped up in pseudo-evangelical language and justification, few people have realized what was happening.'[5] Elsewhere, he makes this frank admission: 'The rock music industry is perhaps one of the most corrupt in existence, and the unthinking transfer of its techniques to the Christian sphere has resulted in some of the uneasy mixtures of gospel and garbage which have in the past gone under the name of "gospel concerts".'[6]

Motives under the microscope

Those are serious statements – and they are made by
someone who knows the Christian pop music scene from
the inside – but let us be as positive as we can and assume
that the vast majority of those in the gospel pop scene are
sincere Christians seeking to serve God through gospel
music. What reasons do they give for believing that they
are right in doing so?

1. 'It draws the crowds'
There is certainly no question about that. The huge
crowds that attend pop gospel concerts easily out-
number those attending gatherings centred on preaching. But should that surprise us? In the first place, pop
music has become an indispensable part of today's youth
culture. Many teenagers are immersed in their music. It
is an identity mark – and the gospel pop event gives the
young Christian an opportunity to express his Christianity in this way without resisting the pressure of his
cultural group.

Secondly, Christian pop makes no spiritual, moral or
ethical demands. It is essentially presented as entertainment, something to be enjoyed – and pop gospel musician John Allen knows where that leads: 'It seems undeniable that most of the audience is there simply to enjoy
the music, not to think hard about anything; and there is
a real danger of the emergence of the "Greenbelt Christian", the semi-converted, shallowly committed teenager whose Christianity means little more than that he
enjoys festival-going.'[7] That is a very significant admission even if, as Allen claims, the organizers are
aware of the problem.

Thirdly, we are living in a time of spiritual depression,
when the church has a much greater appetite for the
trivial and amusing than for the biblical and searching. If

we are honest, A. W. Tozer's words have an undeniable ring of truth about them: 'It is scarcely possible in most places to get anyone to attend a meeting where the only attraction is God.'[8] But that must never be an excuse for conceding to man's lack of spirituality. As Paul Bassett says, 'One of the subtlest ways of flattering man is to communicate the gospel in a way he wants rather than the way he needs.'[9]

Having said all of that, the claim about popularity is irrelevant, because our real concern should be with truth and principle, not voting figures.

2. 'It communicates to young people in a language they can understand'

Here, in a letter to *Evangelical Times,* is an example of the way in which this argument is put, with an attempt to back it up by Scripture: 'We believe that many young people would switch off their minds if presented with a message in Radio 2 or Radio 4 style, but would at least give Radio 1 type presentation a hearing. We believe that the presentation of the gospel through the medium of contemporary music, Radio 1 style, will bring the gospel to the ears of many who might otherwise not hear it. We believe this echoes Paul's statement, "I have become all things to all men so that by all possible means I might save some" (1 Corinthians 9:22).'[10]

What do we say to this? Our first comment would be that the biblical quotation has been wrenched completely out of context, because it comes from a passage in which Paul is focusing attention on *the primacy of preaching,* not suggesting that he is open to a limitless number of alternatives! That being said, there is no doubt that pop music *does* communicate, and that what may seem to be disjointed lunacy to 'golden oldies' is a definite language to the 'in' crowd. Like all other music, pop is bound up with its culture – in this case the culture of the young – and there are times when its language is virtually unintelligible to others.

Taking all this for granted, the big question is whether pop music communicates the *gospel* in this way. We maintain that it does not, for the crucial reason that the medium has a distorting influence on the message. David Hesselgrave makes this point very powerfully in a statement which does not have pop music particularly in mind: 'Missionaries must divest themselves for ever of the naïve notion that the reception of the gospel message is the same irrespective of how it is conveyed to the world – whether by book, magazine, radio, television, film, sound recording, etc. Perhaps no fiction has had wider currency than if you put a gospel message into any of these media at one end, it will come out at the other end as the same message . . . *The media must always affect the message.*'[11]

To return to pop music: does *this* communicate the gospel effectively and without distortion? After all, it is vitally important that the message of the gospel is not only biblically given but biblically received. Now the Bible's primary appeal is to the *mind:* God says, 'Come now, let us *reason* together' (Isaiah 1:18); Christ's summary of the First Commandment includes the need to 'love the Lord your God . . . with all your *mind*' (Mark 12:30); Paul makes it clear that the way to prevent conformity to the world is 'by the renewing of your mind' (Romans 12:2). Yet, as Graham Cray, former Chairman of the Greenbelt Committee, admits, 'In all pop music lyrics are secondary. Pop is music of feeling, spoken primarily to the body and only secondarily to the intellect.'[12]

That is a very significant statement – made by an expert in the field – and it is backed up by singing superstar Larry Norman: 'In order to decide whether

Christian music has any great weaknesses or strengths you have to decide what its purpose is. If it's for non-Christians – to convince them that Christ is an important alternative to seek in their life – then most Christian music is a failure because *it doesn't convincingly communicate that particular message.*'[13]

These statements become even more significant when we put them alongside others from the Greenbelt stable. Graham Cray summed up the 'Greenbelt principle' by saying that 'Some evangelical parents send their children to Greenbelt because they know they won't be preached at. Greenbelt's evangelistic power is its indirectness.'[14] That kind of statement would be serious enough (with its veiled inference that preaching is something from which our young people ought to be protected!) but as far as Greenbelt is concerned even indirectness seems to be giving way to something more disturbing. An editorial in *Strait,* the Greenbelt magazine, asked, 'What if we started inviting bands to play at Greenbelt who have "no Christian stance" but who are significant artistic contributors to contemporary music, no doubt bringing pleasure to their own creator whether they recognize it or not?' But how can performers with 'no Christian stance' bring pleasure to their Creator when the Bible plainly says, 'Those controlled by the sinful nature *cannot please God'*? (Romans 8:8).

There is another and much more important point to be made here and that is that the Bible makes it clear that the unconverted man *cannot* understand the gospel: 'The man without the Spirit does not accept the things that come from the Spirit of God, for they are foolishness to him, and he cannot understand them, because they are spiritually discerned' (1 Corinthians 2:14). Not that this gives us an excuse for sitting back and doing nothing. We must do all we can to communicate clearly, forcefully and persuasively – but at the end of the day only the Holy Spirit can carry the truth into the mind, the heart, the conscience and the will. So to say that the unconverted teenager 'understands gospel rock' is a dangerous half-truth. He may understand rock (whatever may be meant by 'understanding' it) but he certainly doesn't understand the gospel.

3. 'Music is essentially neutral and is coloured only by the words'

This is undoubtedly one of the strongest arguments put forward in favour of gospel rock – and we must therefore give it very careful attention. These two statements summarize what is being said. In Larry Norman's words, 'The sonic structure of music is basically neutral. It's available to anyone to express any kind of message they choose.'[15] To quote John Fischer, 'Basically, music is neutral. Art forms are neutral.'[16] In a private discussion, one of today's pop gospel superstars suggested to us that the first music heard on earth might have been a raindrop falling on a tautly-drawn leaf. He then suggested that as that was neutral and created by God all music was both neutral and God-given. But to jump straight from a raindrop to a rock concert and to lump them together with everything in between is frankly naive. It is obvious that a single *note* (dictionary definition: 'a tone of a definite pitch')[17] does not of itself have any influence, good or bad. It has neither message nor meaning. In that sense, we agree that it is 'neutral'. But the debate is not about single, isolated notes, but about *music* (dictionary definition: 'the art and science of combining tones in varying melody, harmony, etc. so as to form complete and expressive compositions').[18] The words 'expressive compositions' are important – they tell us that when single notes or tones are deliberately brought together in a musical work they are no longer neutral. When music is composed, it is not composed into a neutral nothing, but into a positive something – a form that is definite and meaningful, with colour and character.

We can illustrate the same principle by comparing music to the printed word. The text of Psalm 23 in the New International Version has 437 letters of the alphabet. Before they were assembled by the printer, these letters were neutral. They were complete and perfect, but they meant nothing, they had no message. But in Psalm 23 they have been grouped together to form an expressive composition. Now they *are* saying something, and the order in which they have been composed precisely determines what they are saying.

Take those same 437 characters, arrange them differently, and instead of spelling out a message of assurance, comfort and faith for the Christian believer they could spell out a message of hate, greed or violence. Compose them in some other way and they would form a shopping list. The individual letters would be the same, but they would have lost their neutrality in the composition. The American popular scientist Benjamin Franklin once said that with twenty-six lead soldiers he could conquer the world. The lead soldiers were the letters of the alphabet and Franklin's point was that when assembled together in the right numbers and in the right order they had power to change men's lives. Once assembled, the soldiers would no longer be neutral – nor are musical notes and tones when assembled into an expressive composition.

The point is so important that it is worth listing a number of statements to back up our contention that music is not neutral. Firstly, let us listen to some comments on music in general, spanning centuries of time. Plato (428–348 B.C.), the outstanding Greek philosopher, wrote, 'Musical training is a more potent instrument than any other, because rhythm and harmony find their way into the inward places of the soul.'[19] Elsewhere he contended that music could strengthen a person, or cause him to lose his mental balance, or to lose his normal willpower so as to render him helpless and unconscious of his acts.[20] Aristotle (384–322 B.C.), Plato's most famous student, wrote, 'Music has the power to form a character.' Boethius (c. 480–c. 524), the Greek philosopher and statesman, wrote, 'Music is a part of us, and either ennobles or degrades our behaviour.'[21] John Calvin (1509–1564) wrote, 'We know by experience that music has a secret and almost incredible power to move hearts.'[22] Coming to the present time, one authority after another could be quoted along the same lines. To repeat words we quoted earlier from Sheila Ostrander and Lynn Schroeder: 'The idea that music can affect your body and mind certainly isn't new . . . The key has always been to find just the right kind of music for just the right kind of effect.'[23] Cyril Scott adds this: 'Music affects the minds and emotions of mankind. It affects them either consciously or sub-consciously, or both. It affects them through the medium of suggestion and reiteration. It affects them either directly, indirectly, or both.'[24] Dr George Stevenson, Medical Director of the National Association for Mental Health, Inc., says, 'The widespread occurrence of music among widely distributed people and various cultures is evidence that in music we have a great psychological force.'[25] Dr Howard Hanson, Director of the Eastman School of Music at the University of Rochester, says, 'Music can be soothing or invigorating, ennobling or vulgarizing, philosophical or orgiastic. It has powers for evil as well as for good.'[26] As an everyday illustration of this, Dr Glenn Wilson, a University of London psychologist, says that music and heartbeat are interrelated: 'Muzak is music at heartbeat speed. It creates a warm and relaxed atmosphere which takes your mind off boring work. It puts housewives more at ease when they go shopping, so they are more likely to fill their trolleys up and not worry about the bill.'[27]

Over and above all of these statements, we have the overwhelming testimony of human history, with all its evidence that music has moved man in a hundred different ways. It has calmed his fears, summoned up his courage, soothed his sorrows, stimulated his memory, stirred him to violence, prepared him for death.

There is also a striking illustration of the power of music in the Old Testament, when we are told in 1 Samuel 16 that King Saul called for David to play his harp to him during his recurring bouts of melancholia. We are then told that 'Whenever the spirit from God came upon Saul, David would take his harp and play. Then relief would come to Saul; he would feel better, and the evil spirit would leave him' (1 Samuel 16:23).

To suggest in the light of all that evidence that music is neutral and has no message is frankly absurd.

But what about rock music, which is our primary concern? Does it share this kind of influence? Bob Larson has no doubts about that: 'Teenagers are immersed in their music, and their philosophies are being formed by the lyrics, the call to action in the beat, and the personal opinions of rock idols . . . On occasion I have been accused of overstating the effect of rock music. Many sociologists, however, now believe that there is no other factor doing more to influence teenage folkways, values and morals . . . we of the mass communications generation live under the unprecedented influence of a formidable formulator of human thought.'[28] Professor Frank Garlock agrees: 'No other single influence has done as much to shape the standards and moral conduct of today's teenagers as rock 'n' roll.'[29] Writing in *The*

Guardian, Cedric Cullingford speaks of schoolteachers' reactions to pop music, and says, 'Of all the mass media, pop is the one that is most often cited by them as influencing children.'[30] Later on in the same article he writes, 'In a study of nearly 500 children it was clear that their tastes changed very rapidly according to the state of play of *Top of the Pops*.'[31]

We have stressed this particular point because the issue is tremendously important in considering the whole subject of rock music and the gospel. We leave it with these clinching words by Dr Max Schoen, in his book *The Psychology of Music:* 'Music is the most powerful stimulus known among the perceptive senses. The medical, psychiatric and other evidence for the non-neutrality of music is so overwhelming that it frankly amazes me that anyone should seriously say otherwise.'[32]

One further point: if music is neutral, if it can say whatever the hearer wants it to say, then why are certain kinds chosen as background music played on aeroplanes, in supermarkets, or in places likely to be stressful? If music is neutral, why would we consider the theme music from Alfred Hitchcock's film *Psycho* unsuitable to be played in dentists' waiting rooms? The obvious reason is that the music is chosen *to do something*; and the reason it can do something is that it is not neutral.

4. *'There is a distinctive difference between Christian rock and secular rock'*

This argument is strongly advanced by some of those with interests in the religious pop scene, but other thoughtful observers disagree. Rock singer Chuck Girard, for instance, makes this honest admission: 'If you took the lyrics away and changed them to a secular message, I don't think you would be able to tell the music apart from pop, rock-orientated music.'[33] In 1973 Steve Turner reported in *Buzz,* 'The difference between a Slade concert and many Jesus rallies is negligible.'[34] Eight years later Professor Verna Wright reported that when gospel and secular rock records were played in a controlled test held in a Belgian youth club, the hearers 'couldn't tell the difference'.[35] This exactly confirms the contention of Dr William J. Shafer, who says, 'Rock is *communication without words,* regardless of what ideology is inserted into the music,'[36] and of Professor Frank Garlock, who says, 'The words only let you know what the music *already says . . . The music is its own message* and it can completely change the message of the words.'[37] What all of this is saying is that rock music is rock music, not just a plastic medium that can be bent in any direction. Even John Fischer, who believes that music is neutral, admits that 'Some art forms have been created to express certain philosophies *and are so wedded to those philosophies that they convey that kind of outlook.*'[38] Even more significantly he adds, 'We can't assume that we simply plug in a Christian message and everything will be okay.'[39]

Surely it is not difficult to relate this to today's pop gospel scene? Perhaps these words by Richard Taylor sum up the fatal flaw in the argument that religious rock is somehow different: 'We cannot change the basic effect of certain kinds of rhythm and beat simply by attaching to them a few religious or semi-religious words. The beat will still get through to the blood of the participants and the listeners. Words are timid things. Decibels and beat are bold things, which can so easily bury the words under an avalanche of sound.'[40]

5. *'It produces excellent results'*
It certainly seems to. The popular Christian press

reports dozens and sometimes hundreds of 'decisions' registered at a single pop gospel event and the immediate, visible results from road-show religion seem to relegate the effect of straightforward preaching to that of a badly beaten also-ran. But is that the whole story – or even the *real* story? Let us dig behind the headlines.

In the first place, the pragmatic argument is simply not valid. We gladly accept the sovereignty of God in salvation, and do not deny that in his gracious wisdom he has saved young people and others in gospel rock concerts – but the fact that God uses any means is not of itself any indication that it is biblically valid. As Franky Schaeffer points out, in condemning poor quality in Christian art forms, 'The excuse that "sometimes people are saved" is no excuse at all. People have been saved in concentration camps because God can bring good from evil, but this does not justify the evil.'[41]

God is God and can use anybody and anything for any purpose he chooses – but his use of them does not make them right. God used the Egyptian ruler Ramases II as an instrument in releasing the entire nation of Israel from slavery in Egypt – and told him in the process that 'I have raised you up for this very purpose, that I might show you my power and that my name might be proclaimed in all the earth' (Exodus 9:16). Yet Ramases II was a godless tyrant and certainly not an example for us to follow. Moses got excellent results when he struck the rock at Meribah-Kadesh and produced enough water for the entire Israelite community and all their livestock, but God condemned and punished him for what he did. In all the varied reaction we have had to earlier editions of this book, we have yet to come across anyone willing to take up this point with us. *The general silence on this issue says a great deal!*

We need to learn and relearn the lesson. The pressure

to produce has eaten deeply into the fabric of the church and, as Eric Wright puts it, 'The evangelists' methods and the results they perceive have become the theology of evangelism . . . and woe betide the one who tilts at this "sacred cow".'[42] But we *must* tilt at it, and constantly remind ourselves that every aspect of evangelism must be ruled by biblical principles. In Dr J. I. Packer's words, 'When evangelism is not fed, fertilized and controlled by theology it becomes a stylized performance seeking its effect right through manipulative skills rather than the power of vision and the force of truth.'[43]

Let us take a look at the results said to be produced by pop gospel evangelism. Do they bear close examination? To try to assess this, we explored them in three areas.

In the first place, we conducted a census among 1,829 young people in England, Wales, Scotland and Northern Ireland between the ages of fourteen and twenty-five (the group most thoroughly exposed to the pop gospel idiom), asking them to indicate the circumstances in which they were converted or the major influence in their conversion. The young people concerned came from churches of seven major denominations in both urban and rural areas. Some of the churches were specifically involved in the pop gospel scene, others were not. The poll indicated that of the 1,829 young people concerned, only thirty-nine, or 2.1%, were converted at a gospel concert. (Even this tiny figure almost certainly gives an exaggerated picture; the poll did not ask whether the musical presentation was the specific means of conversion.)

When these figures were first published, one critic suggested that they might conceal more than they reveal because no indication was given as to how they compared with figures and percentages for other influences in people's conversion. This was a fair point, so we went

back over all the response forms – and discovered that
gospel concerts produced the lowest total of conversions
in any of the eleven categories we listed. To give some
examples, Sunday School or Bible Class, evangelistic
campaigns and youth camps were each five times more
productive, while church services and personal conversation were each the major influence in about ten times
the number of cases.

Secondly, we tried to obtain what we might call a
'middle-term' assessment of the results claimed by the
religious road shows that have toured Britain during the
past two years or so. This proved somewhat difficult, as
in many cases figures are not available. However, we do
know of an instance in which over 200 'decisions' had
dwindled to four by the time a follow-up meeting was
arranged a few weeks later and of others where the leak-
age had been just as serious. In the same general area of
road-show religion we know of a school at which 100 'decisions' were recorded in the course of a band's 'ministry' there – yet a short time later the only lasting effect
seemed to be that one of the students concerned showed
'a mild interest' in Christian things.

Thirdly, we wrote to eleven major missionary
societies (chosen in alphabetical order from the UK
Protestant Missions Handbook) asking for an indication
of how many of their candidates had been converted or
called into full-time Christian service in a pop gospel
context. Here are the relevant extracts from their
replies.

'From our experience we have not had any missionary
candidates approach us for service who have come to
know the Lord through such means.'

'We have found few, if any, people who have come to
faith through this sort of musical presentation.'

'I cannot call to mind anybody who has been converted through this type of youth evangelism and has subsequently gone on to missionary service.'

'Over the years I have interviewed quite a number of men for the mission and I cannot recall any one of them indicating that the Christian pop scene has been at all influential in their conversion or Christian life.'

'I certainly do not know of anyone who has come into the mission through the musical pop scene.'

'None of our candidates appears to have been converted in the sort of atmosphere you describe.'

'As far as we can tell, we have not had any candidate who has been converted through this kind of evangelism.'

'I do not think that we have sent anyone to the field whose conversion during the last five years could have been attributed to evangelical road shows.'

'We have not had any applicants for missionary service over the past five years who were converted through entertainment evangelism.'

'The simple answer to your question is "No".'

'As far as we can tell none were converted at such meetings.'

Another missionary society which heard about our enquiries wrote, 'We have nobody amongst our candidates (and at the moment we have about thirty-five) who were influenced by pop concerts.'

In addition, we received the following unsolicited note from a minister who knew of our enquiries and who had until recently been closely connected with a major missionary society not included in our sample: 'You may be interested to know that I spent ten years majoring in candidate interviewing and selection. I recall not one incident of a pop concert featuring in a conversion or call. It may have, but I recall none and in recent years I was more alert to this possibility.'

The heavy emphasis on music as a vehicle for presenting the missionary challenge may well be a contributing factor to the disturbing statistic that the outflow of overseas missionaries from the UK fell by about 1,000 in the years 1976–1986.

These facts and figures are not only disturbing but alarming. The pop gospel scene in Britain today is a high-powered, multi-coloured, glossily packed, heavily promoted industry – but it seems that when the music stops, the applause dies down, the lights go out, the cash is counted and the show moves on, what is left is only a microscopic fraction of what seemed to be. When there is that kind of difference between the headline and the bottom line, something, somewhere, is seriously wrong. It is time to strip the bandwagon down and start again.

7.
Square one

Discussion on a controversial subject can begin almost anywhere – with a news item, perhaps, or a well-known person's opinion, or an obvious change in trends. But for the Christian there is one fundamental principle that should govern all his thinking and ultimately determine his decisions.

Anything from God?

About 589 B.C. a man called Zedekiah was the puppet king of Judah, then held in captivity in Babylon. He was a nasty piece of work, and we are specifically told that neither he nor any of those he influenced 'paid any attention to the words the Lord had spoken through Jeremiah the prophet' (Jeremiah 37:2). He even allowed Jeremiah to be imprisoned on a trumped-up charge of trying to desert to the Babylonians. But when the going got really tough he sent for him and asked him this crucial question: 'Is there any word from the Lord?' No doubt the place was buzzing with all kinds of rumours and speculation. There must have been dozens of theories as to the cause of Judah's problems, and just as many as to what the solution might be. But when the chips were down Zedekiah knew in his heart that there was only one thing that mattered: *what does God say?*

It's in the book

For today's Christian, Zedekiah's question can be put like this: 'What does the Scripture say?' (Romans 4:3). The Christian is not left at the mercy of his feelings on matters of either belief or behaviour. God has not only spoken but has caused his words to be written down for us to read, study, understand and obey. In the Bible's own words, 'All Scripture is God-breathed and is useful for teaching, rebuking, correcting and training in righteousness, so that the man of God may be thoroughly equipped for every good work' (2 Timothy 3:16). This means that the Christian should come to the Bible not as a *last* resort (ransacking it to find statements which he hopes will back up his own opinions) but as a *first* resort, so that his views will be grounded, governed and guided by a word that 'stands firm in the heavens' (Psalm 119:89).

Many of the great Christian leaders over the centuries have expressed this submission to Scripture in memorable ways. Augustine, who died in A.D. 430, yet remains one of the most influential Christians in history, once said, 'We must surrender ourselves to the authority of the Holy Scripture, for it can neither mislead nor be misled.' Martin Luther wrote, 'Before the Word everyone must give way.' John Calvin said, 'The Bible is the sceptre by which the heavenly King rules his church.' And John Wesley claimed, 'I am a Bible bigot. I follow it in all things, both great and small.' Yet we must not think of that kind of philosophy as being the special achievement of spiritual giants. This is *normal* Christianity. Opinions are interesting, trends are significant, arguments are fascinating, but the Christian must be governed by God – and that means being governed by Scripture. As the seventeenth-century preacher William Gurnall said, 'The Christian is bred by the Word and he must be fed by it'! The Christian who is determined to begin at square one must put away his newspapers and magazines and sit down with his Bible.

Five hundred plus

Trying to find a specific reference to particular subjects in the Bible is sometimes like trying to find the proverbial needle in a haystack. (Not that that makes those references unimportant; God does not have to repeat himself for his words to have authority.) What is more, some important subjects are mentioned surprisingly seldom: for instance, there are no more than four references to the Lord's Supper in the whole of the Bible. When we come to the subject of music, the situation is quite different. The Bible contains no fewer than 550 references to music, musicians and musical instruments, and our problem is not where to find them but how to assemble and understand them.

In the beginning – singing stars

Although the Bible is scientifically accurate, it is not a scientific textbook, and its accounts of the creation bear this out. They are extremely brief and sometimes almost lyrical. For instance, speaking of the creation of the world, God asks Job,

'On what were its footings set,
   or who laid its cornerstone –
while the morning stars sang together
   and all the angels shouted for joy?'

(Job 38:7).

No doubt the phrase about stars singing is metaphorical, but surely it is also *meaningful*? If God can speak of the pure response of his created works to the majestic glory of his creation in terms of song, surely singing must be something which God welcomes and in which he delights?

That's an order!

We can confirm God's approval of music by noticing the many times when the inspired writers of Scripture *command* his creation to praise him in song. Here are some examples:

> 'Let the heavens rejoice, let the earth be glad;
>   let the sea resound, and all that is in it;
>   let the fields be jubilant, and everything in them.
> Then all the trees of the forest will sing for joy;
>   they will sing before the Lord'
>
> (Psalm 96:11,12).

> 'Let the rivers clap their hands,
>   let the mountains sing together for joy;
> let them sing before the Lord'
>
> (Psalm 98:8).

> Praise the Lord, all his works
>   everywhere in his dominion'
>
> (Psalm 103:22).

Again, however metaphorical all this may be, it is clearly something God ordains and desires, and if these were the only biblical references to music and singing we had they would be sufficient for us to know that music has a God-given place in his universe.

All people that on earth do dwell

If stars and trees, mountains and rivers are told to praise God, we should surely expect to find the same response demanded from man, the crown of God's creation – and we do, on page after page. Here are just some of the dozens of instances we could quote:

> 'Sing to the Lord, you saints of his;
>   praise his holy name'

> (Psalm 30:4).

> 'Sing joyfully to the Lord you righteous;
>   it is fitting for the upright to praise him.
> Praise the Lord with the harp;
>   make music to him on the ten-stringed lyre.
> Sing to him a new song;
>   play skilfully, and shout for joy'

> (Psalm 33:1-3).

> 'Shout with joy to God, all the earth!
>   Sing to the glory of his name;
>   make his praise glorious!'

> (Psalm 66:1-2).

> 'Sing to the Lord!
> Give praise to the Lord!'

> (Jeremiah 20:13).

These references are nearly all in what we might call a 'general' context, but many others are more specific, with people being told to sing praise to God for his goodness to them in particular circumstances, for special blessings received, for deliverance from their enemies, and so on. Even more important than the context is the *focal point* of all this worship, praise and thanksgiving,

which is *God himself*. In fact, God and the praising
music of his people are so wrapped up together that
Moses and the Israelites could sing, 'The Lord is my
strength *and my song*' (Exodus 15:2). As they celebrated
their miraculous deliverance from the hands of the
Egyptians, their song of praise had God not only as its
object and inspiration, but as its theme. In the fullest
possible sense, they sang to the glory of God.

God's gift

Another factor we must note, in this general look at the
place of music in Scripture, is that music is not only *for*
God but *from* God. In praising God for delivering him
from a difficult situation, David says, 'He put a new song
in my mouth, a hymn of praise to our God' (Psalm 40:3).
Even that one reference is important! It tells us that it is
not enough to think of music merely in terms of human
culture but of divine creation. Music is certainly an art,
but it is primarily a *gift*. As John Calvin once put it, 'All
arts proceed from God and ought to be held as divine
inventions.'[1] Elsewhere he goes on to say, 'Among other
things adapted for men's recreation and for giving them
pleasure, music is either the foremost, or one of the prin-
cipal; and we must esteem it a gift from God designed for
that purpose.'[2] A number of years earlier Martin Luther
said the same thing more colourfully: 'Music is to be
praised as second only to the Word of God because by
her are all the emotions swayed . . . When natural music
is sharpened and polished by art, then one begins to see
with amazement the great and perfect wisdom of God in
this wonderful work of music . . . He who does not find
this an inexpressible miracle of the Lord is truly a clod
and is not worthy to be considered a man!'[3] We agree

with them both. No Christian can legitimately be
opposed to music *per se*. He may prefer one style or type
to another, but to reject music out of hand is to oppose
God's intention for him, and to be less than the whole
person God wants him to be.

The farmer, the musician and the toolmaker

There are those who believe that the first reference to
any subject in the Bible is of particular importance, and
this would certainly seem to be so in the case of music. It
comes just a few generations removed from Adam and
Eve, when the Bible tells us about the three sons born to
Lamech and his two wives, Adah and Zillah. This is how
they are introduced: 'Adah gave birth to Jabal; he was
the father of those who live in tents and raise livestock.
His brother's name was Jubal; he was the father of all
who play the harp and flute. Zillah also had a son, Tubal-
Cain, who forged all kinds of tools out of bronze and
iron' (Genesis 4:20-22). That sounds like nothing more
than part of somebody's family tree, but there is much
more to it than that. These three brothers were obviously the 'founding fathers' of three important groups of
people. The first was a farmer and the third a toolmaker
– and agriculture and industry are obviously vitally
important for man's well-being. But the middle brother
was a *musician*, with the obvious inference that man is
more than just a food-eating worker. He has other
dimensions beside the physical and material – and the
needs of one of those other dimensions are properly met
by music. In the words of the American classical pianist
Sam Rotman, 'Here, within the compass of but a few
verses, God reveals that the provision of man's material
needs is not enough; in addition, man must have an outlet

for his aesthetic sensitivities. Even from the beginning music was more than a mere pastime which could be viewed as something pleasant but essentially unnecessary. Simply stated, God has created in man a certain aesthetic need which can be best satisfied in music, and in his love and wisdom he has provided for this need.'[4]

Music is not merely something that is potentially pleasant; it is something essential to the total needs of total man – and God has lovingly provided man with the ability to exercise his gifts in order to create it. The picture is simple and beautiful. The very existence of music should cause us to praise the God who gave it to us.

Feelings and faith

We ought at this point to ask ourselves one very basic question about music: *what is it for*? Put very simply, the answer is that music is one of the ways by which man can give audible expression to his common emotions – joy, sorrow, love, sympathy, heroism, compassion, and so on – and as we turn the pages of the Bible, beginning with the Old Testament, we find it used in all of these areas. In Erik Routley's words, 'Music was in very wide use in the culture of Israel at all its stages . . . we can distinguish epics and dirges in secular contexts (insofar as any context for Israel was secular), and songs of praise, thanksgiving, instruction, personal experience, and liturgical significance in the religious context.'[5]

Yet most Bible references to music occur in direct connection with the worship and service of God; with man's religious faith rather than with his 'general' feelings. The first of these references is in Exodus 15, where we have the great 'freedom song' of Moses and the Israelites. By the time we reach 1 Chronicles religious music has become highly sophisticated and organized,

with King David appointing no fewer than 4,000 singers
'to praise the Lord with the musical instruments I have
provided for that purpose' (1 Chronicles 23:5) and 288
master musicians 'trained and skilled in music for the
Lord' (1 Chronicles 25:7).

Nor must we forget that the Psalms formed a
'hymnbook' for Old Testament believers, with some of
the instructions (which are part of the text of Scripture)
being quite specific in giving details of the musical instruments to be used. Psalm 4 has the note, 'with stringed
instruments', and Psalm 5 'for flutes' – presumably to
ensure that the music matched the words. What fascinating 'forewords'! God was not to be worshipped in a slap-
dash way. Great care was taken to meet certain criteria.

The point is important, because many of those
involved in gospel music today would point back to the
highly organized music of the Old Testament and claim
that it gives them all the licence they need for 'doing
their own thing' – but closer examination tells a different
story. It has been pointed out that of the eight musical
instruments in use by the Israelites, only four (harp,
lyre, cymbal and horn) were specifically authorized for
use in the temple. Timbrels were taboo, as were flutes,
pipes and dulcimers – though these are mentioned in the
Psalms and could properly be used elsewhere. What is
more, the musicians had to come from certain families,
play only on limited and special occasions, and only at
specific times during the service. There was no question
of a free for all, with anyone who could play an instrument being invited to join the band and turn the service
into a music festival. Instead, music was rigidly controlled in the temple worship, presumably to ensure it
was never the predominant factor. The broader lesson is
that neither in music, nor in any other area of life, has
God given us licence to 'do our own thing'.

What happened to the hyssop?

But the pop gospel musician who tries to lean on chapter
and verse in the Old Testament has further problems,
because if he continues reading his Bible he soon discovers that all of that musical organization was a purely temporary arrangement. It was part of the Old Testament
ritualistic and sacrificial system that was abolished by the
death of Christ. All the paraphernalia of temple worship, though ordained by God, was part of a system of
types, figures and shadows that was done away with
when Christ instituted the new covenant. Those who justify their musical activities purely on the grounds that
musical instruments were used in Old Testament worship could find the same justification for putting tassels
on their clothing, asking God to purge them with hyssop,
walking about Zion and waving bits of dead rams!
Would it not be more biblical to agree that all of these
types, systems, rituals and sacrifices (ordained by God
to accommodate the particular spiritual darkness of Old
Testament times) have now been abolished, and
replaced by the simple beauty of Christ's statement that
true worshippers are those who worship 'in spirit and in
truth'? (John 4:24).

The New Testament

What is extraordinary about the 500 musical references
in the Bible is that they are virtually all in the Old Testament. The other remarkable division we must note is
that of all the New Testament references, only ten or so
refer to Christians here on earth (the others being to the
heavenly hosts mentioned in Revelation) and of these
two are quotations from the Old Testament. Of the
remainder, two merely tell us that Jesus and his disciples

sang a hymn before they left the Upper Room to go to Gethsemane (Matthew 26:30; Mark 14:26); one that while in prison at Philippi, Paul and Silas were 'praying and singing hymns to God' at midnight (Acts 16:25); and another that Paul was determined to sing God's praises in a language that could be understood by the hearers (1 Corinthians 14:15). There was 'music and dancing' in the parable of the prodigal son (Luke 15:25), while James gives the simple instruction: 'Is anyone happy? Let him sing songs of praise' (James 5:13).

That leaves just two places in the whole of the New Testament where there is direct instruction given on the subject – and they are parallel passages, saying virtually the same thing. Writing to the Ephesians, Paul says, 'Speak to one another with psalms, hymns and spiritual songs. Sing and make music in your heart to the Lord, always giving thanks to God the Father for everything, in the name of our Lord Jesus Christ' (Ephesians 5:19). Writing to the Colossians he says, 'Let the word of Christ dwell in you richly as you teach and admonish one another with all wisdom, and as you sing psalms, hymns and spiritual songs with gratitude in your hearts to God' (Colossians 3:16).

Notice the identical lists Paul mentions: psalms, hymns and spiritual songs. What were these? 'Psalms' would be mainly, but perhaps not exclusively, the Old Testament Psalms as we know them; 'hymns' would be current compositions in praise of God the Father and the Lord Jesus Christ (we may have snatches of some of these here and there in the New Testament); while 'spiritual songs' seemed to have covered a rather wider range of lyrical compositions, but could have included the other two groups.

And that's it! The New Testament has nothing else to say on the subject. Yet even these brief phrases have lessons for us. In the first place, variety is encouraged in

Christian worship. As Derek Kidner puts it, 'Our garden
of praise, if we may put it so, is not to be all vegetables,
or even all one kind of flower.'[6] Secondly, however,
variety does not mean licence to do anything we please.
'Psalms' and 'hymns' had direct reference to God, but
the songs, too, had to be 'spiritual' – an important qualification. Music about God should reflect his glory,
beauty, holiness and order, and should direct men to
him and to his ways. Thirdly, as the nineteenth-century
preacher and commentator Albert Barnes wrote, 'The
prevailing character of music in the worship of God
should be *vocal*. If instruments are engaged, they should
be so subordinate that the service may be characterized
as *singing*.'[7]

Each of these principles is important. The Bible says
we are to do 'all for the glory of God' (1 Corinthians
10:31) – and we do not do this by merely tacking God's
name on to something, any more than adding 'in the
name of Jesus' to a prayer makes it audible in heaven or
effective on earth. To use music for God's glory is to use
music that draws attention to him, that mirrors his
majesty, and that meets all the biblical criteria we have
before us. Quite apart from anything else, this means
that we should take any composition of words or music
to Philippians 4:8 and ask these questions: 'Is it true? Is
it noble? Is it right? Is it pure? Is it lovely? Is it admirable? Is it excellent? Is it praiseworthy?' If it fails to meet
these standards, we have no right to use it in God's
service.

Eloquent silence?

Before we leave our look at music in Scripture, there is
one final point to make – one which may at the end of the
day prove to be the most decisive of all. In all of the Old

Testament references, there is not one instance of music being used to help communicate Judaism to the heathen. There is no record, for instance, of the Israelites organizing a Jewish religious folk festival to try to convert the Hittites, Hivites, Jebusites or Amalekites! Even more significantly, there is no reference in the New Testament to the early church using music to reach non-Christians with the gospel (though music was obviously available to the church). All the references are to the church at worship; there are none to the use of music in evangelism.

Surely that is very striking? Here is the church, bursting with new life, longing to tell the world about the risen Christ. Here are its Spirit-filled leaders, willing to give everything, even their own lives, to reach men and women with the gospel. Here is the apostle Paul saying, 'I have become all things to all men so that by *all possible means* I might save some' (1 Corinthians 9:22). Yet we never once read that they used the powerful medium of music to get their message across. Did they miss the boat – or did they know something we have either forgotten or ignored?

Of course, there are those who will say, 'But that is an argument from silence.' Yet if we are absolutely honest we have to ask ourselves this question: is the silence saying something – something crucially important?

8.
Yours sincerely, Concerned

When the American evangelist D. L. Moody visited Scotland for his great evangelistic campaigns in 1873 his partner was Ira D. Sankey, whose organ playing and singing attracted great crowds. But when the team went to hold a Sunday afternoon service in Glenorchie Church, Edinburgh, church leaders took one look at the organ and said, 'We're no havin' such a kist fu' o' whistles in our kirk,' and promptly dumped it out on to the street! When prejudice is in control reasoning is usually rationed!

Throughout this book we have tried to give *reasons* for everything we have said. We are not 'knocking' music, not even pop music as a whole, *but we are concerned.* We are concerned for the glory of God, which should always be the ultimate aim of every Christian. We are concerned for the good of the church, all of whose members are our brothers and sisters in Christ. We are concerned for the integrity of the gospel; we don't want to see it dragged in the mud. We are concerned for the spiritual welfare of young Christians, who are sometimes so cynically manipulated by an older generation. In this chapter we want to 'earth' some of these concerns in certain areas of pop music evangelism.

What's the difference?

Firstly, we are concerned that the pop gospel idiom can

so easily encourage *worldliness*. To find out what we mean, read these two paragraphs.

'This is music to hit yourself on the head to. Who cares if the lyrics are a bit simple, even banal in places? The album runs from solid rock through to electric blues and ends up at heavy metal. There are times when the female vocalist sounds like Janis Joplin and at others her voice is like wailing banshees in the night.'

'They're the sort of people that my mother told me not to play with. I bet they spit on buses! You won't like this album if you're any kind of weed . . . It's that nasty, noisy, loud heavy metal stuff. Not unlike Quo. Very roots rock 'n' roll. Sounds in places like lunatic music. Exciting, throbbing, subversive rock 'n' roll – just like it should be. Can you describe head-banging as intellectual? . . . Good stuff – buy it!'

Where do you think those quotations are from? *New Musical express? Sounds,* perhaps? Wrong and wrong, in that order! They came from the Christian youth magazine *Buzz.* The first is a review of the album 'Barnabus' by Hear the Light.[1] The second is a review of a record by a band called 100% Proof.[2] Yet in the same issue Scripture Union has a full-page advertisement including them in 'twelve of the best' records currently available.[3]

Here is an advertisement for another group: 'Ear smacking, flame quenching, hot-rocking, light showing, different sounding, health damaging, gospel telling, crowd pulling – *Rock Salt.*'[4] Substitute 'story' for 'gospel' and that could be an advertisement for the most vulgar or destructive band playing today. Only one word separates it from that – and our concern is that the difference *is* no more than a word and that the spirit is the same as that of the world. That ridiculous hype may be good promotion, but is it *scriptural*? We get the same picture in the Greenbelt literature. Here is a report on the group Tense: 'Their huge visual assault and presence engendered an electric atmosphere. The visual pinpoint is the girl singer, clad in black, bending low like a stalking animal, or standing still, head thrown back. "The Bunker Song" was a perfect showcase for her evident talent, the full-bodied voice sweeping low over the music, almost snarling, bringing an icy edge to the song.'[5]

Here is another collection of quotations along the same lines. *Buzz* wrote of the Barrett band, 'It's bold and classy and never gives you a minute's peace. It is power-packed and positively bursting at the grooves'; while Steve Taylor's six-track mini LP was said to be 'the most exciting and radically prophetic recording the rock 'n' roll subculture has so far presented to the church . . . There is no hint of Scripture-spouting religiosity here.' *Strait* reported that at Greenbelt 'Mark Williamson's Band played their usual highly organized chaos of a funk set with every conceivable gag thrown in.' Record reviews in *21st Century Christian* included those on Tramaine, 'the black dance album, with a synth bass and percussion sound hard enough to rattle your teeth . . . Don't quibble, get dancing . . .'; and Kev Adrian, 'a crisp set of electro-pop songs which bubble and throb with dazzling danceability'.[6]

Without making any judgement on the sincerity or integrity of anyone involved, the question we want to ask is this: what kind of *spirit* does all of this suggest? Doesn't it seem to be one which is merely aping the world? Is this spiritual and helpful or sensual and unhelpful? To avoid being misunderstood, let us make it clear that we are not making a distinction between spiritual and *physical*. Man is body, mind and spirit and all can be engaged in spiritual activities. The Bible

makes this perfectly plain: 'Offer your bodies as living
sacrifices, holy and pleasing to God – this is your
spiritual act of worship' (Romans 12:1). The question we
are asking is whether a religious cloning of show-
business presentation makes it spiritual or leaves it as it
was – worldly. There is a difference between being
animated and anointed. As Bob Larson rightly puts it,
'Clothing and choreography will never make the gospel
appealing. Great men of the faith have been martyrs,
not swingers.'[7]

Let us take this a little further. The Bible makes it
clear that we are not to dress or behave in ways that
might create moral problems for other people. When
'secular' singers do so, we are right to condemn what
they do. Then can we excuse the Christian pop star when
he unbuttons his shirt, wears skin-tight leather trousers
and wiggles his buttocks at the audience? What is the difference? Do the 'Jesus words' in the songs sanctify his
actions?

This highlights one of the greatest problems in Christian pop, the fact that it blurs the gap between Christian
and non-Christian value systems by trying to incorporate
them both. The difficulty of marrying rock/pop music to
a biblical message can been seen in a *21st Century Christian* review of an album called 'All Systems Go' released
by Donna Summer, the former raunchy pop star who has
professed conversion. The review runs, 'It's a good
boppy record with a dash of Christianity. Messages
range from the subtle to the not so subtle – don't sleep
around, live for God, etc. There is also some great dance
music on one side.'[8]

Richard Peck, who spent twelve years playing and
recording rock music, and then went into the music pub-
lishing business, also has some perceptive things to say
about the problems of combining the rock/pop idiom
with the gospel message. He cites Amy Grant, one of

America's most popular gospel singers. One of her best-known songs is 'I Love A Lonely Day', but as Amy Grant told a radio interviewer, the listener could apply the message of the song 'to any relationship he or she chooses'.[9] Perhaps this blurring of the message is understandable in her case, because as she said elsewhere, 'I'm a singer, not a preacher . . . I'm not trying to convert anybody.'[10] Then what *is* the work of the *gospel* singer? Is conversion not a primary goal in communicating the gospel? One can hardly imagine a preacher getting away with that kind of statement!

Peck also cites Donna Summer in illustrating the problem. He says that her song 'Unconditional Love' has 'nominal Christian lyrics', but 'focuses on a fuzzy, non-discerning "love" that could keep Christians from exhorting men and women to come out of their sin'.[11] He adds that Donna Summer's duet with Matthew Ward of the group Second Chapter of Acts 'shows love between a man and woman as causing them to abandon all control'.[12] He also points out that Steve Taylor's song 'Jenny' tells of a girl who fell into sin and committed suicide. Are these Christian values? Are they communicating the gospel?

U2

Sometimes the gap between performance and reality is downright tragic. U2 is undoubtedly one of today's 'mega-groups', with record sales reaching into the millions. Their 1987 LP 'The Joshua Tree' became the fastest-selling album of all time and launched them into an orbit that reinforced their claim to be the top rock band in the world. The following year their 'Rattle and Hum' productions were among the year's major musical talking points.

What is more, the accolades are not all secular. Dave

Roberts of the Christian Musical Association said, 'They
are . . . the most profound Christian contribution to the
pop culture in the last forty years.'[13] Elsewhere, Roberts
went further. After a Greenbelt concert, early in U2's
career, he enthused over their 'October' album: 'The
record commands us to rejoice, and that's exactly how I
feel when I hear it. It is so full of biblical truth it is like
having a Bible study every time I listen to it.'[14]

So far so good – but an article in *Melody Maker* gives
a radically different picture. Interviewed in Dublin by
Ted Mico, lead singer Bono said, 'I'm going to destroy
the whole f . . . . . . [expletive deleted] U2 myth, the U2
godhead . . . Every . . . [expletive deleted] thing I say
becomes some sort of statement, something of vast
importance. I could go on stage, unzip my pants and . . .
[vulgarity deleted] on stage, and people would think that
it was some statement about something or other.'[15]

Adam, another member of the band, was no more
sanctified in his statements: 'Spirituality and sex are so
close. If you try and have sex without spirituality, it's not
sex. Isn't that just the difference between a . . . [expletive
deleted] and making love? One is an exhausting one-
night stand and the other an inexhaustible union. That's
what we saw in that roots music. The prim and proper-
people call it gospel music, but the people who know
what it's all about call it sex music, because that's what it
is.'[16] The impact on the interviewer was significant: 'If
you're thinking of reaching for that brown paper airline
bag by the settee, remember that U2 are not the only
people to find a chord binding carnal pleasures and
celestial promise. "Lovesexy" is Prince's name for
God.'[17] Is this kind of verbal filth part of what Dave
Roberts calls 'the most profound Christian contribution
to pop culture in the last forty years'?

Who's number one?

Our second concern is that rock music evangelism encourages *exhibitionism*. Writing a number of years ago in the old British Youth for Christ magazine *Vista,* Ben Ecclestone, in an article entitled 'Rape of the Ear', said, 'All musical performance carries with it a built-in temptation to put on an act,' and there is no doubt that he is right. Provided one isn't petrified with fear, there is something powerfully attractive about going on stage in front of a crowd. We know this to be true as evangelists and believe the danger to be even greater for musicians, whose appeal is so much more directly to the emotions.

Exhibitionism is basically one area of worldliness and rock musician Keith Green was in no doubt that many Christian artists had failed to get it right. In *Can God use Rock Music?* he wrote, 'Frankly, I have been just as much offended by most of what I've heard and seen as any sweet ole Christian grandma who accidentally stumbles into a blaring-loud gospel concert . . . It isn't the beat that offends me, nor the volume – *it's the spirit*. It's the "*look at me!*" attitude I have seen in concert after concert, and the "Can't you see we are as good as the world?" syndrome I have heard on record after record.'[18]

This tendency to act as stars instead of servants is clearly reflected in the kind of advertising and review material published in the popular Christian youth press. For example, the following comments all appeared in one issue of *Buzz*: 'A fantastic feast of rock and praise'; 'the finest Christian music'; 'leading Christian artists'; 'highly talented newcomers'; 'unbelievable'; 'British Christianity's biggest, most energetic and certainly loudest event'; 'top stars'; 'extraordinary entertainment'. *Buzz's* successor, *21st Century Christian,* publishes

advertisements with a similar avalanche of adjec-
tives. Here are words from two placed in the January
1988 edition: 'Martyn Joseph Band with special guest,
celebrating the launch on Pulse Records of new albums
. . . A mega-stage production . . .'. 'Get caught in it!
Fifty-one hours of the finest in Christian rock music,
drama, teaching, worship, fellowship and fun explode
the myth. From mainstage you'll be under decibel attack
from rock acts like Martyn Joseph . . . and the righteous
reggae of Ben Okafor . . .'

How does that kind of language tie in with the apostle
John's statement that 'Everything in the world – the
cravings of sinful man, the lust of his eyes and *the boast-
ing of what he has and does* – comes not from the Father
but from the world'? (1 John 2:16). Is it not also faintly
ridiculous? To make the point, we have taken three
advertisements from *Buzz* and substituted our own
names for those of the musical performers. This is the
result: 'John Blanchard is one of Britain's most popular
Christian preachers. His personality, distinctive oratory
and powerful sermons are now world famous. His most
recent sermon, "How I found humility" looks destined
to reach the very top for style and popularity'; 'What
stimulates the grey cells, gives your feet a treat and does
your ears a favour? All of those who answer "Heineken"
leave the room immediately. The answer is Peter Anderson, with his multi-media sermon entitled "Whose side
are you on?"'; 'Derek Cleave has the distinction of being
a catalyst for some of the best preaching performances in
the world. His achievements and experiences as part of
the famous Christian Ministries team is clearly evident in
the way he preaches.' Would that kind of nonsense be
acceptable in advertising our meetings? If not, why not?
And if not, why should it be acceptable in any part of
God's service? The apostle Paul's approach was exactly
the opposite: 'For we do not preach ourselves, but Jesus

Christ as Lord, and ourselves as your servants for Jesus'
sake' (2 Corinthians 4:5).

Any honest Christian knows that genuine humility is
hard to come by. Fighting pride is a constant and costly
struggle. To a greater or lesser extent we all have an
appetite for appreciation, a liking to be lauded. Assess-
ing musicians on the basis of how professionally they
perform in playing and singing about the one who deliberately 'made himself nothing, taking the form of a servant' (Philippians 2:7) is not only unhelpful to all concerned but a total contradiction of a central truth of the
Christian faith. Keith Green wrote very powerfully on
another aspect of this: 'Why are we so star struck? Why
do we idolize Christian singers and speakers? . . . Can't
you see that you are hurting these ministries? They try
desperately to tell you that they don't deserve to be
praised, and because of this you squeal with delight and
praise them all the more. You're smothering them . . .
crushing their humility and grieving the Spirit.'[19]

Dr Alan Redpath, one of the 'senior statesmen'
among British evangelical preachers, puts his finger on
the spot in his book *Blessings out of Buffetings:* 'The
principle of the world is "self-glorification" and the principle of the Christian is "self-crucifixion". The principle
of the world is "exalt yourself" and the principle of the
Christian is "crucify yourself". The principle of men is
greatness, bigness, pomp and show; the principle of the
cross is death . . . There is never a breaking through of
communication of [Christ's] life in your heart and
through you to others in heavenly conviction and
authority which will challenge or bless them unless at
that point there has been a personal Calvary.'[20] The
application of this to the pop gospel performer is surely
not difficult? One of the inherent problems about the
idiom is that the attention is focused firstly on the singer
and then on the song – whereas the object of evangelism

is to get the attention focused on the Saviour. We can
come at this from another angle. When trying to convey
a verbal message to someone, it is *unnatural* to back up
the words by swaying, squirming, dancing, slinking or
gyrating various parts of one's anatomy. When these
things are done on stage they are an act, part of a show
– and showmanship on the part of a gospel communicator (preacher or singer) is an abomination. His
sole duty is to point people to Christ; to draw attention
to himself not only fails to help in getting the gospel
across, it positively hinders any attempt to do so. It also
places the performer in a dangerous position in the light
of God's very clear statement: 'I will not yield my glory
to another' (Isaiah 48:11). There is no questioning the
fact that the pop gospel idiom encourages exhibitionism.
In Michael Green's words, 'What we need is not just a
message of crucifixion, but the crucifixion of the
messenger.'[21]

On with the show?

The third concern we have is that gospel is presented as
entertainment. This is undoubtedly one of the 'crunch'
issues on the whole subject and we will therefore need to
look at it thoughtfully, carefully and *honestly*. Let us
begin by getting our definitions clear.

Firstly, what do we mean by *'entertainment'*? The
verb 'to entertain' has at least twelve different mean-
ings,[22] but we can soon whittle the list down. Five are
now obsolete and can immediately be dropped; again,
'to entertain' can mean to provide food or shelter, to
treat hospitably, to take something into consideration,
to hold something in the mind, or to meet or experience
something – none of which really applies here. That

leaves us with three: 'to hold the attention or thoughts of', 'to hold the attention of pleasurably' and 'to amuse'. We suggest that it would be perfectly fair all round to say that neither the first nor the third of these fits the gospel pop bill. On the one hand, music's primary appeal to the emotions makes the first definition somewhat exaggerated; on the other hand 'to amuse' is commonly associated with making fun, and although some gospel pop performers do take unbiblical liberties in that area, it would be unfair to tar them all with the same brush. That leaves us with 'to hold the attention of pleasurably'. To use the dictionary's noun, 'entertainment' in this sense is 'a performance or show intended to give pleasure'[23] – and we suggest that that is a perfectly fair description of pop gospel evangelism.

Secondly, what is the *gospel*? As every Christian knows, the word simply means 'good news', but it is important to remember that it is not good news about the possibility of a better life-style or how to solve life's problems; nor even about the possibility of shaking off a guilt complex and 'feeling great'. Essentially, the gospel is good news about a *Person,* the Lord Jesus Christ. In what were possibly the first New Testament words ever written, Mark calls it 'the gospel about Jesus Christ, the Son of God' (Mark 1:1). The apostle Paul constantly refers to it as 'the gospel of Christ' (Romans 15:19; 1 Corinthians 9:12; 2 Corinthians 2:12; 9:13; 10:14; Galatians 1:7; Philippians 1:27; 1 Thessalonians 3:2). The insistence is important! There is no gospel apart from Christ, there is no gospel without Christ and there is no gospel outside of Christ. Elsewhere, Paul calls it 'the gospel of the glory of Christ, who is the image of God' (2 Corinthians 4:4). An 'image' (or likeness) is something that can be seen, and Paul's words emphasize the point that the gospel is a combination of who Christ is and what Christ did. These are the essential elements of the gospel – *and there is nothing entertaining to be found in any of them.*

If not one single element in the gospel message is entertaining, how can the gospel possibly be presented as entertainment? The life of Jesus was not a religious road show; he did not come to give a performance, but to give his *life*! At the end of the day, this is the fatal flaw in entertainment evangelism – it is a contradiction in terms. The object of entertainment is to give pleasure (and there is nothing essentially wrong with pleasure), but the object of evangelism is to warn man of his appalling spiritual condition and to point him to the one who 'came into the world to save sinners' (1 Timothy 1:15). As Paul Bassett rightly says, 'The danger is just as great today as it was in Paul's day of producing a crossless Christianity whose flattering appeal creates fans, but not followers.'[24]

The whole thing becomes even more absurd when we realize that although the gospel is good news, it does not appear so to the sinner. The Bible speaks of 'the offence of the cross' (Galatians 5:11); it describes Christ as 'a stone that causes men to stumble and a rock that makes them fall' (1 Peter 2:8); it says that 'The message of the cross is foolishness to those who are perishing' (1 Corinthians 1:18) and that the message of a crucified Saviour is 'a stumbling-block to Jews and foolishness to Gentiles' (1 Corinthians 1:23). To the unconverted, the glorious message of the gospel is sheer nonsense; to tell him that his only hope of the forgiveness of sins and eternal life lies in the hands of a young Jew who was murdered and rose from the dead 2,000 years ago insults his intelligence, offends his sense of decency and hurts his pride. Then how can we do these things and *entertain* him at the same time?

All of this underlines the seriousness of the work of evangelism. The apostle Paul could tell the Ephesians, 'I served the Lord with great humility and with tears' (Acts 20:19) and 'I never stopped warning each of you night and day with tears' (Acts 20:31). Can the evangelistic entertainer honestly claim to have that kind of burden? In the work of evangelism, the church is a lifeboat, not a showboat!

(Perhaps we need to put a paragraph in parenthesis here. In pointing out the fundamental folly of entertainment evangelism we are not suggesting that the Christian message is one of gloom and doom, best presented by people with personalities and styles to match. After all, the Bible says that 'The kingdom of God is not a matter of eating and drinking, but of righteousness, peace and joy in the Holy Spirit' (Romans 14:17). But the order of those key words – 'righteousness', 'peace' and 'joy' – is not accidental. The Christian life is certainly meant to be one of *joy,* but a Christian's real joy depends on the extent of his *peace* (of heart, mind and conscience), while his peace depends on his *righteousness* (his right relationship with God). To offer joy before peace, and peace before righteousness, is to put both carts before the horses. There is never true joy without peace and no real peace without righteousness. So the *first* aim in evangelism is not to bring joy (let alone superficial happy feelings) but to bring home to people the need to get right with God. As Dr Martyn Lloyd-Jones said, 'The business of preaching is not to entertain but to lead people to salvation, to teach them how to find God.'[25])

Artists or ambassadors?

Larry Norman, one of the best-known performers ever to appear on the pop gospel scene, has virtually admitted the impossibility of combining entertainment and

evangelism. Asked, 'What is the main aim of your ministry?' he replied, 'I don't think music is a ministry. Music
is just a bunch of notes.'[26] Later in the same interview,
when asked what he was trying to achieve through his
music, he said, 'I *never* achieve evangelism through my
music. If I'm going to say anything evangelistic, I say it
with words and not music. Music is art, not propaganda.'[27] Larry Norman's honesty is helpful. Pop music
aims at pleasing people, evangelism aims at saving them.
Pleasing people is a perfectly legitimate aim, of course –
in the right context. Holiday Inn, the international chain
of motels, call themselves 'The People Pleasin' People'
and no doubt they have countless satisfied customers to
say that that's fine. But pleasing people must never be a
factor in evangelism. One of the principles that governed New Testament evangelism was this: 'We must
obey God rather than men' (Acts 5:29). Paul could say,
'We are not trying to please men but God, who tests our
hearts' (1 Thessalonians 2:4) and a moment later, 'We
were not looking for praise from men' (1 Thessalonians
2:6).

This poses a constant and fundamental problem for
the gospel pop singer. He *is* trying to please men, but the
idiom he is using is one that imposes what we might call
'popularity pressure' – *his* popularity. The publicity, the
spotlights, the presentation, the applause – all the attention is on him rather than on his message. When John the
Baptist was preaching, his stage was the desert, he wore
his ordinary clothing, his message was clear and uncompromising, he made no attempt to please men and his
attitude was one of utter humility. We might almost say
that it was the most natural thing in the world for him to
point to Jesus and say, 'Look, the Lamb of God' (John
1:29). It is almost impossible for the gospel pop singer to
have that same spirit, because of the pressures the idiom

imposes on him. However sincere his motives, however genuine his personal devotion to the Lord, whatever his songs are saying, what so often comes across is not 'Look, the Lamb of God', but 'Look at *me* saying, "Look, the Lamb of God".' His real dilemma is put in a nutshell by David Porter when he says, 'The problem is that art was never meant for preaching with at all.'[28]

Keith Green once wrote that 'The only music ministers to whom the Lord will say, "Well done, good and faithful servant" are the ones whose lives prove what their lyrics are saying, and the ones to whom music is the least important part of their life – glorifying the only worthy One has to be the most important.'[29] How many of today's Christian 'stars' give the impression that they are meeting those criteria?

David Wilkerson is internationally known as the author of the best-selling book *The Cross and the Switchblade* and for founding the drug rehabilitation ministry Teen Challenge. There was a time when he was quoted in support of the validity of rock music as a medium for communicating the gospel, but he is subsequently on record as having thought his position through from a biblical perspective. Now he has started a ministry called Times Square Church, located adjacent to Broadway in the heart of Manhattan. Although his services are held in a theatre and entertainment district, *Evangelical Times* reports that 'None of those elements is evident in David Wilkerson's meetings.' The ET report goes on to say this: 'He recently walked out of a Mylon Le Fevre "contemporary Christian music" concert saying, "I was horrified by what I saw. I saw demonic images rising from that stage: I heard Satan laughing!" And on 1 October he made his convictions perfectly clear: *"We've had enough joy-pop religion."*'[30]

The shallow end is dangerous

Our fourth concern is that entertainment evangelism can
so easily reduce the gospel message to *triviality*. This
comes across in a great deal of the advertising for gospel
concerts and the like. To speak about 'star-spangled
entertainment' and 'extravaganzas' (we quote from
Buzz) may bring in the crowds, but the language is a far
cry from Gethsemane and Golgotha.

The pop idiom also tends to trivialize the message. To
give one simple example, 'You can't keep a good man
down' may be a very 'pop' way of singing about the
resurrection of Christ, but it is theologically trivial and
biblically criminal. Countless other gospel pop songs are
equally trivial in content, not only as far as the doctrines
of God are concerned, but also those concerning man's
response to the gospel. Graham Kendrick admitted this
when speaking at Spring Harvest: 'One of my criticisms
of those of us who use music in evangelism is the nature
and content of the "gospel" which is preached. All too
often, a superficial kind of believism is offered, along
with promises of large helpings of love, joy and peace.'
He then went on to suggest that the triviality was not
only in the songs but in the singers: 'One can only
assume that many of us preach this because our own
commitment or understanding of discipleship is superficial.' Even more revealingly, he went on to speak of
those with a 'happy go lucky, anything will do, attitude
towards the business of bringing new spiritual babes to
birth'. Fellow musician Garth Hewitt agreed: 'An
analysis of the lyrics of *most* gospel songs indicates a very
superficial view of salvation and of Christianity.' (The
italics are ours – but the information is his.) When two of
the leading personalities in today's pop gospel scene go
on record as saying that most of the material being used
is very superficial, surely we are right to be concerned at

the sheer triviality that the pop idiom encourages?

The question we want to ask is simple, serious and sincere: is there any valid connection whatever between triviality and Christianity? The point is powerfully made in the following poem, written by a man who before his conversion had moved in the worlds of professional music and drama. He wrote it as his spontaneous response to a visit to Greenbelt:

A few stars speckle the night sky.
Above the cheering crowds, and clapping hands
Coloured balloons float up high, and free.
For whom do the sons of thunder rock the stage?
For whom the spotlights blaze, and colours flash
Like northern lights – flooding over the fields?
Shall Christ come with a dizzy dance now?

Or shall he come – somehow differently
Dove-winged on the eddies of the air?
The thunder mumbles words I cannot hear. . .
A shrill microphone, a heavy beat,
But the still, small voice is lost in a cloud
Of sound. Christians wear their carefree smiles,
Then one man and his guitar take the stage:

Shut the door, keep out the devil – he says
And sings, as the spirit lifts among the balloons.
Surely we clap and cheer for this now! . . . ? . . .
But the Lord of life remains back stage it seems.
Shall the name of Christ pale, and dwindle away?
The tents are pitched like Israel round about,
The stalls are stacked with books to teach us how. . .

To bring a cause for peace philosophy.
Through the crossfire of disharmony
The drama and the dance unfold themselves

While learned men bring words like offerings –
The religious world would bring us radical change.
For whom do the sons of thunder rock the stage?
Shall the name of Christ pale, and dwindle away?[31]

The truth or the tune?

Our fifth concern is that reliance on the pop gospel idiom
betrays *a lack of faith in the gospel*. If the idiom has so
many weaknesses and dangers, why go on using it? The
argument of many is that young people will not listen to
the gospel presented in any other way. Youth leaders
and others have said as much to us: 'We'll need to get a
band, or the young people won't listen. Music is the only
way we can reach them.'
     Is that true? Is there any other *serious* subject that we
would insist needed to be communicated by music
before it could be understood and accepted by young
people? Imagine an eighteen-year-old employed by a
company that insists on an annual medical check-up for
all its staff. He seems very fit and has no sense of need,
but goes reluctantly to hospital when his time comes.
After a careful examination, the doctor discovers that
the young man is suffering from a serious disease that
will prove fatal unless he receives immediate and radical
treatment. Can you imagine the doctor asking his assistant to set the man's disease to music, rustle up a few
nurses, plug in some musical instruments and then get
them to sing the diagnosis to the patient – *because that
would be the best way to get through to a teenager*? The
idea is absurd – yet time and again we are told that you
must have music before young people will listen. We
could extend the illustration: if the pop music medium is
so effective at communicating to young people, why not

use it in schools, colleges and universities? Why not give biology some beat, jazz up geography, get into heavy metal history and liven up languages by doing them in a disco? The reason is obvious and the same in each case: the medium does not fit the message. As an expert in the pop gospel field has admitted to us, 'Music does not lend itself to presenting the facts of the gospel in the ordered, sequential way which is to be required if there is to be a thoughtful response.'

This being the case, let us ask some straightforward questions. Is it true to say that it is the *unsaved* who insist on the music? Or is it nearer the truth to say that it is young *Christians* who enjoy it so much that they insist on it? Is it true that unconverted friends of Christians adamantly refuse to attend any evangelistic presentation except a musical one? Or is it truer to say that they are almost never asked? Isn't it true that young Christians invite friends to gospel concerts as a first resort rather than as a last resort? When told that music was the only way to get through to young people today, an evangelist friend of ours replied, *'Have you never heard of the Holy Spirit?'!*

The pop idiom has virtually become a life-support system for youth evangelism in Britain today, and we believe that one of the reasons for this is that Christians have lost that naked faith in the power of the gospel that was the hallmark of the early church. Dr Alan Redpath made the following comment to us on this particular point: 'The growing tendency to the sensual appeal of rock music is one of the tragedies of our time. People tell us that the church has lost touch with the world. That is nonsense. The fact is we have lost touch with *God,* and when we do that we resort to every possible alternative to put on a programme, one of which is the very heavy slant towards rock music. It is the outcome of wrong priorities in the church. We will not see revival as long as we offer Christian entertainment to people. The Holy Spirit is not in that business.' If that diagnosis is right, then a great deal is wrong!

Messiah with blow-waves

Our sixth concern is that the pop idiom *tends to water down the gospel*. In his book *The Divine Conquest*, A. W. Tozer writes, 'If I see aright, the cross of popular evangelicalism is not the cross of the New Testament. It is, rather, a new bright ornament upon the bosom of a self-assured and carnal Christianity. The old cross slew men; the new cross entertains them. The old cross condemned; the new cross amuses. The old cross destroyed confidence in the flesh; the new cross encourages it.'[32] In *Of God and Men* he adds this: 'Much that passes for New Testament Christianity is little more than objective truth sweetened with song and made palatable by religious entertainment.'[33] Those are serious charges, but we believe them to be true. Of course, Tozer is referring to church life in general, but his comments particularly apply to the popular music scene. There are essential elements of biblical truth that cannot be fitted into the narrow and shallow confines of a pop gospel idiom. Can a pop song explain what is meant by God, sin, judgement, the death of Christ, faith or justification? And if not, how can it convey the gospel? Geoff Thomas goes so far as to say, 'It is impossible to communicate the gospel of Romans in music, dance or drama.'[34] The pop gospel approach has another problem in this area: doctrines such as the sovereignty of God, the depravity of man, the substitutionary death of Christ, the need for genuine repentance and the call to holiness of life cut and hurt and offend the natural man. He *hates* these things. How

then can they possibly be conveyed to him in an entertainment idiom, which is designed to be pleasurable to
his senses? You cannot touch a man's heart by tickling
his ears. Dr J. Sidlow Baxter makes this comment in his
book *Rethinking our Priorities:* 'Pop style, lilty, swingy
airs or strummings simply do not fit the rich, deep,
urgent, serious truths of the Bible and the gospel.'[35] In
other words, the music does not fit the message. The
music may be popular, but as Erik Routley says, 'If any
music is composed or performed with an eye simply to
attracting the unconverted, it is likely to fall into the
same error we find in the parson who, in order to make
users of bad language feel at home, uses bad language
himself.'[36]

One of the results of trying to convey the whole biblical picture by pop music is that you end up only conveying part of it – which means that the listeners receive a
fragmented message instead of a full one. All too often
the end result is that people *do* enjoy hearing the 'gospel', because it has been tailored to suit their wants
rather than to meet their needs. They are quite happy to
'make a decision for Christ', because the Christ they
have heard about is not the Christ of Scripture – he is the
kind spoken about by Stewart Henderson (adopting a
persona) in his poem 'Splintered Messiah':

> I don't want a splintered Messiah
> In a sweat-stained, greasy grey robe;
> I want a new one.
> I couldn't take this one to parties;
> People would say, 'Who's your friend?'
> I'd give an embarrassed giggle and change the
>   subject.
> If I took him home, I'd have to bandage his hands.
> The neighbours would think, 'He's a football
>   hooligan.'

I don't want his cross in the hall;
It doesn't go with the wallpaper.
I don't want him standing there
Like a sad ballet dancer with holes in his tights.
I want a different Messiah, streamlined and
     inoffensive,
I want one from a catalogue,
Who's as quiet as a monastery.

I want a package-tour Messiah, not one who takes
     me to Golgotha.
I want a King of kings with blow-waves in his hair.
I don't want the true Christ;
I want a false one.[37]

All too often, that is the one the listener gets. The real
Christ is still 'despised and rejected by men' (Isaiah
53:3). That is what makes him such poor 'box office'.

The hyping of Heartbeat

There was a striking example of the effect of watering
down the gospel in 1987, when *21st Century Christian*
carried a full-page colour advertisement launching the
first single on to the secular market by the Christian
group Heartbeat. The single was called 'Tears from
Heaven/The Only One' and was distributed by RCA
Records. The advertisement said that the object of the
record was 'to bring healing to our nation'. Colin
Urquhart of Bethany Fellowship urged readers to 'buy
the single and broadcast the truth to the nation'. Roger
Forster of the Ichthus Fellowship weighed in by saying
that 'Praising Jesus brings God into society and throws
the enemy out. Supporting this Heartbeat initiative will
contribute to cleansing the spiritual atmosphere of our

country.' Elsewhere, house church leader Gerald Coates reported that Heartbeat had spent almost two years sharing their vision with some fifty national Christian leaders and had got uniformly positive feedback.

In due time, the group appeared on *Top of the Pops*, *The Roxy* and *Smash Hits*. Letters appeared in the February edition of *21st Century Christian* suggesting that the members of the band were probably the country's greatest evangelists to young people.

But much more significant was a lengthy letter from Sue Ritter published in a subsequent edition of the magazine. Sue is a Christian who worked for two and a half years as Assistant Publicity Officer with Radio 1 and Radio 2 and has written many articles supporting the Christian pop scene. Yet her letter included this telling section: 'I was disappointed with Heartbeat. The lyrics of this song were not blatantly Christian. If I wasn't a Christian *I doubt if I would know what they were singing about*. They had the chance to tell the world in no uncertain terms that Jesus died for them. And they blew it.'

Fervent hyping eventually pushed the record into the lower reaches of the charts, but failed to get it played on Radio 1. Why? Because its message was too direct? Not quite! Disc Jockey Simon Mayo told *Strait,* 'To suggest that Radio 1 banned the record because it was "Christian" is nonsense. Radio 1 never even realized that it was "a Christian statement"'!

Focus on the family

Our seventh concern is that the pop idiom *widens the generation gap*. Rock 'n' roll was the first music in the history of the world specifically aimed at the teenage market. Its beat appealed to their awakening senses. It spoke of rebellion, revolution, freedom, independence

– and the more adults objected to it, the more the young took it to their hearts. It became an international anthem for young people and a major factor in establishing the 'youth culture' we have today.

An advertisement placed by Rolling Stone in the *New York Times* said, 'Rock and roll is more than just music. It is the energy centre of a new culture and youth revolution.'[38] In Mick Jagger's words, 'There is no such thing as a secure, family-orientated rock 'n' roll song.'[39] Bob Dawbarn wrote in *Melody Maker,* 'Rock 'n' roll, if not actually inventing the teenager, split the pop followers into the under twenties and the rest.'[40] The Beatles' George Harrison made it clear that alienating adults was no accident: 'Music is the main interest of the young people. It doesn't really matter about the older people now because they're finished anyway.'[41] Prominent music critic George Lees was even more specific: 'Rock music has widened the inevitable and normal gap between generations, turned it from something healthy – and absolutely necessary to forward movement – into something negative, destructive, nihilistic.'[42] Jazz artist Ira Gitler agreed: 'Above all other considerations, rock is definitely the music of today's youth and its importance is more social than musical . . . It sets them apart from the values and attitudes of the adult, establishment world in a more emphatically schismatic manner than ever before.'[43]

It is not difficult to see that philosophy reflected in the life of the church, with young people becoming increasingly segregated from the rest of the congregation. We believe that this tendency to create a 'youth church' is unnatural and unhealthy. The Christian church is a family and the members of a family ought to demonstrate their common solidarity, rather than their differences. In a healthy home all the members of the family eat together, not at different times (unless working hours or other factors require this). Nor is there any such thing as 'youth food'. Nobody markets 'teenage baked beans'. Should there not be a parallel in the church? Of course, we are not suggesting that there should be a law demanding that every Christian should have the same musical tastes – that would be absurd. What we are saying is that rock music has always placed an unnatural emphasis on 'youth culture' as a separate entity in society and that such an emphasis is damaging to the life of the church. This is not empty theorizing; we have seen its effect in countless churches during the past twenty years. Yet there is no such thing as a 'youth church', nor is there a 'youth gospel'. There is '*one* body and *one* Spirit . . . *one* Lord, *one* faith . . .' (Ephesians 4:4-5). Christians are 'all *one* in Christ Jesus' (Galatians 3:28). Nothing should be encouraged which tends to blur that beautiful picture.

Yours sincerely, Concerned

These are some of our major concerns about the pop gospel idiom; there are others which we cannot develop more fully here.

As with other music, gospel rock *tends to blur the need for doctrinal clarity*. For example, an outspoken Roman Catholic can share a gospel concert at the Royal Albert Hall with singers and musicians who are equally outspoken evangelicals. Would the Reformation martyrs have gone along with that?

It *detracts from the unique place God has given to preaching*. As far back as the nineteen-sixties, Ben Ecclestone was concerned enough about the trend to write this in *VISTA*: 'One of the unfortunate tendencies of present-day evangelism is that it has given to gospel beat music an unprecedented place of favour over the preaching of the Word of God. We have been mistakenly led to believe that today, above everything else, we must have music: any music, but beat music in particular. How very far from the truth this is.' The situation is certainly no better today. Preaching has got pushed further and further out of its biblical place, and when that happens to anything we have problems. As David Marshall puts it, 'When preaching in church life retreats before music; to that extent church life itself is retreating from New Testament ground, and moving into the perilous territory of mere human opinion and tradition.'[44] Later in the same article he suggests that where biblical principles are followed, 'music modestly retreats to a subordinate place before the majesty of the Word'.[45]

We also believe that the pop idiom *tends to project a substitute gospel*. A great deal of it concentrates on man's felt needs – his loneliness, emptiness, sadness, lack of fulfilment. The songs then invite the hearers to 'come to Jesus' for joy, peace, thrills, happiness, a 'high'. New Testament preaching never does this; it addresses itself to man's *real* spiritual condition – lost, dead, a rebel, an enemy of God. Man's need is not to get 'turned on' but to get turned around.

This point came across very powerfully in a letter written to us after the publication of the first edition of this book. The writer had been a musician with a Christian rock band when circumstances meant that he began attending a particular church. He goes on: 'For three years I sat under the sound of biblical teaching and those years revolutionized my life. Very soon I learned what the gospel was and as soon as I did so doubts arose in my mind as to the suitability of rock as a medium for the gospel. I spent some months studying the issue and wrote a short essay on my conclusions. My friends could not understand; how unorthodox to suggest that rock music and the gospel are incompatible!

'The reason I think music is used so often in evangelism is because the modern church has a faulty view of the gospel. As soon as the true gospel was shown to me I realized there were serious difficulties in using music to proclaim it, difficulties which you point out very well in your book. What we need among the Christian youth of today is a revival of the true meaning of the gospel. When I saw the seriousness of the gospel I saw the paradox of using a non-serious medium to try to convey it. When the need for repentance is clearly understood from the Word of God it surely becomes unthinkable that such a happy-go-lucky medium as rock is conducive to it. Again, when faith in Christ alone is shown to be indispensable to the gospel we meet the greatest paradox – how can we use a medium where attention (by the very nature of a 'performance') is turned to men, music and lights rather than to the glorious, risen Christ?

'I am convinced that when a young person is brought face to face with the true gospel, then God by his Holy Spirit shows him which methods are and are not usable in its proclamation.

'For years I was involved playing in a band and organizing events where bands would play and not once did I hear the true gospel. Regrettably, I never preached it, and neither did any member of the band. We did not know what it was. The greatest single need of the hour is a return to the true gospel. I am convinced that there are hundreds of young people who trek from one concert to another believing themselves to be converted who, like me, if they heard the true gospel would realize that in fact they are not. The existence of the "Christian rock scene" is a symptom of a great apostasy from the Word of God in our day.'

That is a powerful statement from someone who knows both sides of the argument – from personal experience!

Finally, we believe that the preoccupation of young people with the pop gospel idiom *discourages personal evangelism*. The heavy emphasis on organized events and stage performances tends to turn young Christians into listeners rather than communicators. For countless numbers of them, evangelism has become a spectator sport. Larry Norman certainly recognizes this: 'This whole Christian thing has burgeoned into some dilettante art form . . . The singers are doing one album a year and a lot of concerts and they're so popular. The audience is buying the Album of the Month and making sure their Christian record collection is as complete as required by their tastes. That is not what life is for.'[46]

Let's start again

Many people are sweepingly critical of today's youth. Even within the Christian church there are those who dismiss teenagers out of hand as being so completely caught up in 'doing their own thing' that they are not prepared to listen to a careful examination of issues such as rock music and the gospel. *We couldn't agree less*. As we have spoken to young people while preparing the material for this book we have been very encouraged by their response. Some have been stunned; they had not realized that occultism and other evils had penetrated rock music so deeply; others had never given serious thought to the possibility that, regardless of the lyrics, the music itself is saying something; others have been challenged to become more discriminating about their music. Others have been prepared to go even further, to dismantle their popular prejudices and to take a totally fresh look at their whole approach to music – 'secular' and 'Christian' – based not on the pressures of a worldly youth culture, but on the principles of the Word of God. Our prayer is that this book will help many more to do the same.

9.
Getting in tune with God

Jesus Christ has always had more fans than followers. Many people attracted by his personality, fascinated by his power or impressed by his teaching have never truly submitted to him as the Lord of their lives. That is hardly surprising. The reason most people do not become Christians is not because being a follower of Christ is too soft, but because it is too hard. There are many like the man who said, 'I will follow you, Lord; *but . . .*' (Luke 9:61); not so many prepared to fulfil the basic conditions for discipleship: 'If anyone comes to me and does not hate . . . even his own life – he cannot be my disciple' (Luke 14:26).

Those are not easy terms – but they are simple. Normal Christianity means obedience to Christ in every part of life, whatever the cost. It means setting aside one's own tastes and preferences, likes and dislikes, and submitting every area of life to this one crucial test: *what does Christ want me to do*? He himself put it like this: 'My sheep listen to my voice; I know them, and they follow me' (John 10:27). Nothing could be clearer. The two hallmarks of the Christian are determination to hear whatever God says and to do whatever God commands – to have what Al Martin calls 'an open ear and an obedient foot'!

With that in mind, let us turn specifically to the question of 'Christian music' (which obviously includes the use of pop music in evangelism). What are some of the biblical principles that apply? Before answering that question, it goes without saying that *all* 'Christian music' must submit to the same principles. Personal taste is not the issue. A classical style must keep to the same rules as a contemporary one; the organ and the guitar must be treated alike; the robed choir must be assessed in the same way as the rock group. With that in mind, what principles should govern the music we use in God's service? Perhaps the best way to discover this is to allow us to ask you these questions about the music you write, play, sing, listen to, or use in worship or evangelism.

1. *Does it help you to hear the Word of God clearly?*
The Bible says that 'Faith comes from *hearing the message,* and the message is heard through the word of Christ' (Romans 10:17) and speaks about 'setting forth the truth *plainly*' (2 Corinthians 4:2). The first test is therefore whether the message can be heard – and this must be applied in at least three ways. The first has to do with the *sound* of the music, and with its relationship to the words. After all, it is obvious there is no gospel in the *music.* God gave us the gospel in *words* and nothing in the music must distort or blur or in any way push into the background what the Bible calls 'the word of truth, the gospel' (Colossians 1:5). If the volume or dissonance of the music are such that the words cannot be heard clearly, then the whole performance is an exercise in absurdity.

Here is an example of what we mean. In the course of a 1987 nationwide tour, singer Sheila Walsh visited Worthing, when her show was reported on by *Christian Herald* music editor David Hotton. He wrote quite favourably about some aspects of the evening: 'Sheila relates easily with her audience, speaks helpfully about her faith . . .' But then came the punchline: 'For some of us, however, *communication ended when she sang* because, more often than not, the band was too loud for us to catch the words.'[1] We could not have made our point any better than that!

Can we imagine playing loud or discordant music (or music of any kind) throughout a preacher's sermon in order to help to get the message across?

The test must also be applied in terms of the *character* of the composition. In John Calvin's words, 'We must beware . . . lest our ears be more intent on the music than our minds on the spiritual meaning of the words . . . Songs composed merely to tickle and delight the ear are unbecoming to the majesty of the church and cannot but be most displeasing to God.'[2] Strange as it may seem, it is possible for music to be *too good* to use in Christian worship, because it draws attention *from* the words instead of *to* them. Whatever its style or form, music must always be the servant of the Word of God, never its master. The great Augustine certainly recognized this. In his *Confessions* he wrote, 'I am inclined to approve the custom of singing in church. Nevertheless when it happens that I am more moved by the song than the thing which is sung, I confess that I sin in a manner deserving of punishment, and then I should rather not hear the singing.'[3]

Thirdly, the test must be applied to *the lyrics*. Do they help me to hear the Word of God? Some of our older hymns score heavily here, because they are no more than the Psalms or other parts of Scripture set to poetry and music. The same applies to some modern songs and choruses that have the same basis. But what about other songs? Are they Bible-based? Is the Word of God the thing that gets through? Is there solid doctrinal content? Not all hymnology is good theology.

For an illustration of what we mean, we want to quote

from *Background to the Task*, which was published in 1968 as a supplement to *On the Other Side*, a Report by the Evangelical Alliance Commission on Evangelism. In a section called 'Modern Music and Evangelism' Colin Chapman writes about some of the factors which make it difficult to use pop music to communicate the gospel and at one point mentions the difficulty of using an idiom in which 'love' plays such a large part. He then goes on to say this: 'If we are using an idiom or a medium which in the majority of cases is used to speak about some aspect of love, what effect is this likely to have on the content of the gospel song and on the content of what actually comes across to the listener? Could it be that in using this idiom we have been unconsciously influenced by the associations of the idiom, with the result that when we present Christ in a gospel song we *appear* to be presenting him primarily as a kind of heavenly lover? Could it be that what some of the audience hear is not so much a challenge to come to terms with the God who had made them and to whom they are accountable for their lives, but rather an invitation to fall in love with Jesus? . . . But would we not be more faithful to the gospel if we said that it is our refusal to love God which constitutes the compelling need for us to come to terms with God? . . .'[4]

Chapman's questions still need answering today and they point up one of the greatest dangers in the pop gospel field. As one concerned pastor wrote to us about rock music, 'The medium is so anti-Christian in its ethos – libertarian, anti-authoritarian, equating infatuation and sexual attraction with love, and on the drug-culture fringe – that when Christians assume that ethos to communicate the message of self-denial, cross-bearing and following Christ then it utterly mangles the message.' In an earlier chapter we quoted two leading 'pop gospellers' admitting that the content of most gospel pop songs today is doctrinally inadequate. If that is the case, they fail the first test and we have no right to use them.

2. *Does this music tend to give you a greater vision of the glory of God?*

The first recorded song in Scripture is in Exodus 15 and was sung by Moses and the Israelites to celebrate their miraculous deliverance from the Egyptians. In it are these remarkable words: 'The Lord is my strength and my song; he has become my salvation' (Exodus 15:2). What is remarkable about them is that Moses refers to God as 'my song', and it would be impossible to link the nature of God and the nature of the song more closely than that! God not only caused the song, he characterized it. No wonder Matthew Henry calls it 'a holy song, consecrated to the honour of God, and intended to exalt his name and celebrate his praise, and his only'.[5]

Can the same be said of your 'Christian music'? Accepting that its beat, rhythm and syncopations are saying things, are they things that express the purity, majesty, holiness and serenity of God? Music about God should be like God. It should reflect him, magnify him; it should communicate something of God's character. Does it do this? Is it pure in its tone, lovely in its melody? Fine-tuning the question to the subject of our study, does rock music do it?

Author Jeff Godwin explores one particular facet of this, and points out some other dangers: 'When beautiful harmonies and clear voices of lovingkindness sing "Praise God" in a peaceful and lovely musical arrangement, that's one thing. When snarling, distorted voices yell "Praise God" (like Stryper) over the crash and bang of heavy metal music, two things happen – (1) that good message is obscured by the medium – and why should it be if the words are what really matter? and (2) heavy metal is seen to be "not so bad". In other words, "You can listen to heavy metal as long as it talks about Jesus." This is the same deception that was used when *Jesus Christ Superstar* came out. Either heavy metal is harmless or it isn't – there's no middle ground. How can something be a little evil, or a little good? It's kind of like being a little pregnant, I guess."[6]

The American evangelist David Wilkerson has had a remarkable ministry among drop-outs and other underprivileged young people and is very familiar with today's youth scene. How does he answer the question? In his book *Get your hands off my throat* he says this: 'Christian rock groups are brought to our youth crusades by sponsoring churches. They appear on my stage with their drums and loud guitars, hand clapping their way through songs that speak of Jesus, but with the primitive beat of rock. I try not to act surprised, offended or ashamed. You see, I want so much to relate to these young people. The kids in the audience seem to love every beat. They clap, they smile, they relate, they turn on and they get excited. But something inside me, deep in my soul, does not feel right. There's a small hurt which I can't explain. I feel as though the Holy Spirit within me does not witness to the rock sounds in the middle of a salvation meeting. I also have a sense, an inner knowledge, that the gentle Holy Spirit is not comfortable in the atmosphere this music creates.'[7] Is Wilkerson right?

3. *Does this music tend to give you a repentant view of man's depravity?*

In describing man's spiritual state, the Bible says, 'The heart is deceitful above all things and beyond cure' (Jeremiah 17:9). One of man's most persistent follies is to imagine that whenever he chooses he can pull himself up by his spiritual bootlaces, turn to God, get cleaned up, and become a member of God's family. But that is not the case. Man is corrupt, vile, morally and spiritually rotten to the core. Does your music give you a *repentant* view of all this? The word in italics is all-important. There is certainly a great deal of music that gives a view of man's depravity. Rock music's heavy emphasis on violence, anarchy, rebellion, sexual promiscuity, homosexuality, the drug culture, blasphemy, occultism and the like is saying something that is both loud and clear. One would certainly hope the 'Christian music' would not glorify those things, but neutrality is not enough. The questions we have to ask are these: does it lead you to search your heart and not just to tap your feet? Does it get beyond feelings to facts? Does it make clear to you the reality of man's spiritual condition apart from God?

We have already suggested the great difficulties that any idiom aimed at bringing pleasure has in conveying the 'bad news' that it is vital for man to grasp before he can appreciate the nature of the 'good news'. Does the music you are playing, singing or hearing honestly overcome all those difficulties and do it in such a way that it helps to bring you to a place of repentance, a place where you loathe sin and want to have nothing to do with it?

4. *Does this kind of music encourage you to disciplined, godly living?*

Discovering the details of God's will for his life is the constant concern of every serious-minded Christian, but the overall will of God for him could not be clearer: 'It is God's will that you should be sanctified' (1 Thessalonians 4:3). Yet holiness does not come easily; godliness is never handed to the Christian on a plate. The Christian life is a fight, not a festival; a conflict, not a concert.

It is a constant battle against the forces of evil and calls
for vigilance, discipline, sacrifice and spiritual determination. Does your music tend to lead you in these directions, or does it tend to be soft, slushy or sentimental?
Does it help you to focus your mind on things that are
'true . . . noble . . . right . . . pure . . . lovely . . . admirable
. . . praiseworthy'? (Philippians 4:8). Even more importantly, does the music itself and the way it is performed
enable you to focus your attention on *God* and not on
the performers? Keith Green once wrote, 'I repent of
ever having recorded one single song, and ever having
played even one concert, if my music and (more importantly) my life has not provoked you in godly jealousy
(Romans 11:11) to sell out completely to Jesus!'[8] Does
the music you like flow in that direction?

5. *Does this kind of music help you to separate yourself
   from the world?*

The Bible is crystal clear on the Christian's duty here:
'Do not love the world or anything in the world. If anyone loves the world, the love of the Father is not in him'
(1 John 2:15). That has always been a tall order and
perhaps never taller than in this day and age. Christians
are under siege, pressurized day after day to conform to
philosophies, values, standards and life-styles diametri-
cally opposed to those laid down in Scripture, where we
are told that 'God did not call us to be impure, but to live
a holy life' (1 Thessalonians 4:7) and that as far as these
things are concerned we are to 'come out from them and
be separate' (2 Corinthians 6:17). Yet in his book
Anatomy of Pop, Roy Connolly adds this comment to
the many we have quoted concerning pop music's ethos:
'The notes are only a gateway to a kind of physical and
psychological freedom which human beings find necessary for their survival and sanity. The music is more at
home in the club, the pub and the brothel, in close

association with other group entertainment, drinking and seduction.'[9]

What voice are you hearing in your music? Does it appeal to the sensual or to the spiritual? Does it seem to have its roots in this world or in heaven? Does it stimulate pure appetites or impure? Does it lead you to want more of the world's values, or less? Are godless people comfortable with it or embarrassed by it? Does it help or hinder a desire to break free from the worldly way of doing things? There is no neutrality here – the Bible makes it clear that 'Anyone who chooses to be a friend of the world becomes an enemy of God' (James 4:4). The question is not essentially one of what you like, but of whom you love.

6. *Is this the kind of music that you can imagine being part of a spiritual revival?*

This is a good test, because revival is a time when God himself breaks through in breath-taking power and glory – and therefore a time when we should expect to see an emphasis on those things which have his blessing. The psalmist prayed, 'Will you not revive us again, that your people may rejoice in you?' (Psalm 85:6) – a reminder that revival is sent from God, not staged by man.

What part does music have in such a movement? It has been suggested that music is always strongly associated with every genuine revival, but while this may have an element of truth in it, it certainly needs to be heavily qualified. For example, in genuine revival, music is never prominent as a *performance*. There is certainly congregational singing as God's people rejoice in the Lord, but we are not aware of *any* genuine revival that has centred around a musical 'star'. Surely that is significant?

Wales has had a revival in each of the last three centuries – in 1735, 1859 and 1904. Yet although there were claims of 100,000 conversions at the time, in some places the long-term results of the 1904 revival were comparatively disappointing. For example, it is said that there were 2,000 conversions on Anglesey alone, yet a generation later the island was virtually a spiritual wilderness. Writing in *Reformation Today*, Gwynne Williams suggests some of the reasons for a lack of depth in the work associated with Evan Roberts (the leading preacher of the revival) and says there came a point when he and many of his followers 'lost touch with the essential sanity of New Testament Christianity. Human techniques were used to build up an atmosphere of expectancy; repetitive prayer or *the studied use of music* were especially to the fore.'[10] He then describes his own great-grandfather telling how 'hymns and solos were carefully arranged so as to provide the revivalist with an audience which had been emotionally moved' and adds, 'Incidentally these were the first real examples of entertainment evangelism in Wales, Roberts himself being almost always accompanied by musicians.'[11]

That is a fascinating glimpse into the church's history, but it is more than that. It has often been said that those who will not learn from history are doomed to repeat its mistakes, and the lessons from 1904 can begin to be learned by asking ourselves some questions. Is this music God-centred or man-centred? Does it concentrate on the Lord's glory or on man's feelings? Does it draw attention to the performers or to Christ? Whenever music makes it difficult to see the Son for the stars, we can be sure that there is something wrong!

7. *Is this the kind of music under whose influence you can imagine Christians drawn into sacrificial full-time missionary service?*
Christ's final command to his disciples was to 'go into all the world and preach the good news to all creation'

(Mark 16:15), and it has been said that one of the marks of a church's spiritual health is the measure in which it takes its share in the fulfilment of that commission. It is usually a good sign when a church can point to a steady stream of young people and others who have left the security and comfort of job and home and obeyed God's call to full-time missionary service regardless of the cost, and usually a bad sign when a church has to delve back many years to find the last person who did so. Does this have anything to do with young people's preoccupation with a certain kind of music? Not necessarily, but we feel that some honest questions might be helpful. Does this kind of music appeal to sentiment, or does it touch you at a deeper level? Does it merely encourage enjoyment, or does it lead to evangelism? Does it call you to indulgence, or to sacrifice? Is it music which helps you thoughtfully to count the cost of whole-hearted commitment to Christ? The questions are valid – and the answers revealing! Perhaps another question will help to test where your priorities really lie: how does the amount you give directly to missionary work compare with what you spend on your music?

8. *Would you expect to find this kind of music in heaven?*
Earlier in this book we quoted Martin Luther as saying that the man who did not appreciate music was 'a clod'. We can go further than that and say that the Christian who does not appreciate music is almost a contradiction, because he is on his way to a place where he will be surrounded by music for all eternity! One of the things revealed by God to the apostle John during his remarkable vision on the island of Patmos was that *there will be music in heaven*. In one of the most breath-taking passages in all Scripture we are told about three tremendous songs of praise. The first is where 'four living creatures

and the twenty-four elders . . . sang a new song' (Revelation 5:8-9). Then we are told that 'Many angels, numbering thousands upon thousands, and ten thousand times ten thousand . . . encircled the throne and . . . sang' (Revelation 5:11-12). Finally John tells us, 'I heard every creature in heaven and on earth and under the earth and on the sea, and all that is in them, singing:

> "To him who sits on the throne and to the Lamb
> be praise and honour and glory and power,
>   for ever and ever!"'
>
> (Revelation 5:13).

The first choir has twenty-eight members – four 'living creatures' and twenty-four elders (representing nature and the church?); then they are joined by at least 104,000,000 angels (work it out!); finally by every creature in the entire universe. No wonder Christina Rossetti once described heaven as the homeland of music! But what kind of music is it? Is it music as we know it, with staves and scales, chords and canons? Will there be melody, harmony and rhythm as we know them here? We have no idea. We are not given any details about the music – perhaps to enable us to concentrate on the words. It will certainly be 'a new song' (Revelation 5:9), but as William Freel has said, 'No composer can estimate its value, no instrument can play its harmony, no voice can pronounce its beauty, no modulator can convey its height or its depth; *this song is arranged to please the ear of God.*'[12]

That immediately points us to some important and inescapable questions. Does the music you enjoy suggest that it was arranged for the same ear? Can you imagine it being enjoyed by God the Father? Is it *serious* music? Does it promote a sense of awe and reverence? Can you imagine it being enjoyed by God the Son? Does it give undivided glory to 'the Lamb, who was slain'? (Revelation 5:12). Can you imagine it being enjoyed by God the Holy Spirit? Does it speak of peace, purity and a spirit of worship? There are other questions to be asked, too. Can you imagine this music being played and sung by the angels and archangels, the cherubim and seraphim? Perhaps even more testing is this: can you imagine that when you get to heaven and stand before the indescribable majesty of the triune God of glory this is the kind of music you will want to play and the kind of song you will want to sing?

The apostle Paul says of Christians that 'Our citizenship is in heaven' (Philippians 3:20). That being so, every part of life should be seen as a preparation for that glorious experience. Our music is no exception.

10.
Back to square one

The story is told of a man who, during an election campaign, had a bumper sticker on his car which read, 'My mind is made up – don't confuse me with the facts.' The story has whiskers but it is relevant. As we have seen, the subject of rock or pop music in evangelism is wideranging and complicated, but that has not prevented a great many people (young and old) jumping in at the deep end and delivering their first and last words on the subject without giving it the amount of serious, *honest* thought it demands.

Throughout this book we have tried to be both serious and honest, and to examine the whole subject carefully and courteously, listening to what the experts have to say and keeping personal preferences out of the discussion altogether. We hope we have succeeded, but we would be wrong to leave the whole thing up in the air. Discussion must be followed by direction and decision.

All you have to do . . .

One of the most unusual books in the Bible is Ecclesiastes. Written by an anonymous author known only as 'the Teacher', it is a remarkable commentary on human life and on man's relationship with God. On the last page, we read these words:

'Now all has been heard;
    here is the conclusion of the matter:
Fear God and keep his commandments,
    for this is the whole duty of man'
                                    (Ecclesiastes 12:13).

Of course the 'Teacher' is right. When all is said and
done, man's whole duty consists in fearing (worshipping) God and being obedient to his Word. Someone has
said that loving God is reading the Bible and doing what
it says, and no Christian should disagree with that. Yet
as far as pop music and evangelism are concerned, that
statement makes the issue both clear and unclear! It
makes it clear in that all that is required is obedience:
cultural differences, personal preferences and human
opinions are irrelevant. It makes it unclear in that the
Bible makes no mention of pop music in evangelism.
Where do we go from there?

In his excellent book *Nothing but the Truth,* Brian
Edwards has a chapter entitled 'The Bible, sufficient and
final' in which he says this: 'All matters of doctrine and
life are to be brought to the final test of Scripture. There
are no subjects upon which Scripture has nothing to say
either by *direct command* or *indirect principle* – this is
what is meant by the sufficiency of Scripture.'[1] As far as
pop music in evangelism is concerned, there are obviously no *commands* in the Bible. In fact, as we saw in an
earlier chapter, there are no directions about the use of
any kind of music in evangelism. It is neither commanded nor commended; there is no example of its
being used; it is not even hinted at – and for many Christians past and present that is where the discussion begins
and ends. All the arguments we have brought to bear in
this book would be considered irrelevant. They would
go along with the Puritan preacher John Trapp in saying,
'Where Scripture hath no tongue, we must have no ears,'

and that is a perfectly honourable position to take. Many of the historic doctrinal confessions which surrounded the Reformation did exactly this. The Heidelberg Catechism (1563) said that we were not to worship God 'in any other way than he has commanded in his Word'. The Belgic Confession (1566) said that the Scriptures 'fully contain the will of God . . . The whole manner of worship God requires of us is written in them.' The Westminster Confession of Faith (1646) said, 'The acceptable way of worshipping the true God is instituted by himself' and that God may not be worshipped according to 'the imaginations and devices of men . . . or in any other way not prescribed in the Holy Scripture'. The Baptist Confession of Faith (1689) said that 'The only acceptable way of worshipping the true God is appointed by himself in accordance with his own will . . . and all forms of worship not prescribed in Holy Scripture are expressly forbidden.' Whatever else may be thought, these statements were not drawn up by extremists or cranks, but by our fathers in the faith, those to whom, under God, we owe our Christian heritage today.

If this is your position, reading this book has been purely academic; the silence of Scripture had already convinced you that there is no biblical place for music in evangelism. However, it must be said that a rigid application of this rule (what theologians call 'the regulative principle') does raise massive difficulties in its application to other areas of church life. It buries the 'music in evangelism' issue, but a hundred problems grow on the grave. As we cannot possibly touch on these here, let us turn to the other way of applying the Bible's teaching.

The point about principles

What is the difference between a biblical command and

a biblical principle? Brian Edwards gives a clear and simple illustration in his book. A church which keeps a register of its members is doing something not commanded in Scripture; but there is a biblical *principle* which says that things should be done 'in a fitting and orderly way' (1 Corinthians 14:40), which makes a list of church members sensible and practical. On the other hand, a church which made a charge for membership would be violating a biblical principle; the Bible says that a Christian's giving should be 'in keeping with his income' (1 Corinthians 16:2), and not according to a scale of fees laid down by the church.[2]

How does this apply to pop gospel evangelism? In the course of this book we have sought to bring biblical *principles* to bear on the subject at every stage: in evangelism, words are of paramount importance; nothing must detract or distract from them in any way; any kind of psychological manipulation must be avoided; nothing must be done that will stimulate unwholesome thoughts or appetites; the message must be addressed directly to the mind and not merely to the emotions; the communicator must do everything he can to be obliterated by the message; the message must tell the 'bad news' as well as the 'good news'; the message must be communicated seriously, earnestly, urgently – and so on. *It is our conviction that entertainment evangelism fails to meet these and other biblical principles. It is therefore contrary to the teaching of Scripture and should be abandoned.*

The law of liberty

Although we have tried to present the issue fairly and positively, that last paragraph will sound to some like a prison sentence – harsh, cramping, negative, destructive. Yet if it is biblically sound, that cannot be the case. James calls Scripture 'the law that gives freedom' (James 2:12), while one of the psalmists says, 'I will walk about in freedom, for I have sought out your precepts' (Psalm 119:45). In a nutshell, this means that *the person who is tied to Scripture is set free from everything else* and this emancipation is part of what Paul calls 'the glorious freedom of the children of God' (Romans 8:21). How does this apply to our conclusions? What kind of freedom do you have if you decide to abandon entertainment evangelism? The difficulty in answering the question is not in knowing where to start, but in knowing when to stop.

In the first place, you are free from tradition. It is only in the last hundred years or so that musical evangelism has become a tradition, and in the last thirty years or so that pop gospel has become a tradition within a tradition. Yet you are not bound by either. You have discovered that Christians are called to be true radicals – always linking back to the roots instead of getting caught up in the branches!

On the other hand, you are free from needing to keep in step with the latest style and idiom of gospel presentation. You do not have to be musically 'with it'. You are also free from the risk of turning people away from the gospel because they do not like the style or quality of your music. Recently, Christians at a university told us of some Muslims they had persuaded to attend an evangelistic rally, but had difficulty getting them to stay long enough to hear the evangelist. The reason was the rock music played in the early part of the meeting, which seemed to confirm their worst fears – that Christianity was a Western religion with no message for them.

The Bible asks, 'Who can bring what is pure from the

impure?' (Job 14:4), but you have been set free from the
need to try to wrench your evangelistic music away from
its grubby associations – rebelliousness, occultism,
sexuality, the drug culture and the like.

Christian pop artists invariably imitate the clothing,
gestures, movements and voices of secular performers;
the whole style is set by the world – but you have been set
free from the danger of gospel rock presentations creating or stimulating an appetite for the same kind of music
outside of a Christan framework.

You are free from all the dangers associated with
psychological manipulation in gospel pop, as well as
from the dangers of an emotional response based on the
beat, rhythm and pulse of the music rather than on the
words. You are also free from the serious consequences
of evacuating the message in order to accommodate the
music and from the trivializing of truth which results
from trying to reduce great doctrines to 'pop words'.

In addition, you are free from the twin dangers
associated with the quality of the music – that either the
music is so good or so powerful that it overwhelms the
words, or so poor that the words are condemned along
with the performance.

You are free from the temptation of relying on the
music to 'get results'. A youth group recently pleaded
with us to include a rock band in an evangelistic mission
because 'if we get a band it will make it easier for people
to get saved'. Our answer was to say, 'That depends on
who does the saving!' There was no band (rock or otherwise) on the day of Pentecost when 3,000 were converted, nor in the amazing days which followed, when
'the Lord added to [the church] daily those who were
being saved' (Acts 2:47). You will obviously long for
God to use your evangelistic efforts to bring people to
himself, but you are free to place your unqualified

obedience to his Word above any pressure to produce immediate results.

Finally, and by no means unimportantly, you are free from the embarrassment of needing to explain why so soon after a large number of 'decisions' are recorded, there is so little lasting effect to be seen in the lives of many of those concerned.

The other side of freedom

All the freedoms we have mentioned so far might be called 'negative freedoms': they refer to areas of danger and difficulty from which you are delivered by abandoning entertainment evangelism. But there is another side to freedom. When a person manages to escape through the Iron Curtain he is not only set free *from* Eastern Europe but *into* Western Europe. By abandoning entertainment evangelism you are not only free *from* certain areas, you are also set free *into* other areas.

In the first place, you are free to concentrate much more (as speaker or listener) on *the preaching of the Word of God*. Many Christians have either forgotten or failed to notice the central place that God has given to preaching in the work of evangelism. John the Baptist prepared the way for the coming of Jesus by '*preaching* in the Desert of Judea' (Matthew 3:1). As soon as Jesus began his public ministry he 'began to *preach*' (Matthew 4:17). His final command to his disciples was 'Go into all the world and *preach* the good news to all creation' (Mark 16:15). As a result, we read that 'Day after day, in the temple courts and from house to house,they never stopped *teaching and proclaiming* the good news that Jesus is the Christ' (Acts 5:42). When persecution drove the 'ordinary' church members out of Jerusalem, 'Those

who had been scattered *preached* the word wherever
they went' (Acts 8:4). Paul was crystal clear about his
own commission: 'For Christ did not send me to baptize,
but to *preach* the gospel' (1 Corinthians 1:17). He told
Titus that God had 'brought his word to light through the
preaching entrusted to me by the command of God our
Saviour' (Titus 1:3). Having rejoiced that 'everyone who
calls on the name of the Lord will be saved' (Romans
10:13), he went on to ask these questions: 'How, then,
can they call on the one they have not believed in? And
how can they believe in the one of whom they have not
heard? And how can they hear without someone *preaching* to them?' (Romans 10:14). In a very telling comment
on all this, Geoffrey Wilson says, 'The apostles constantly laboured to inform the minds of their hearers.
They did not exercise a commission to pander to the
basest instincts of the natural man.'[3]

We have lost that emphasis today. As Paul Bassett
rightly says, 'We sing of Christ, recite Christ, dramatize
Christ, but less and less do we preach Christ.'[4] We have
reached the extraordinary situation where the evangelist
has to fight for his place on the evangelistic platform. He
is becoming an endangered species! It would not be an
exaggeration to say that musical evangelism has become
an obsession for many of those involved in youth
evangelism in Britain today. Many would not consider
the possibility of a major evangelistic effort without
employing music as the central feature. In a very real
sense, the medium has become the message. Surely it is
time to turn the tide? In recent missions we have been
very encouraged by the attendance, attention and
response at meetings which concentrated almost exclusively on the preaching of the gospel. We believe that it
is time for those in positions of responsibility to do some
serious, biblical rethinking in this area. The Bible tells us

that when Christ ascended into heaven he made full provision for the ongoing work of the kingdom of God by bestowing various gifts on the church: 'some to be apostles, some to be prophets, some to be evangelists, and some to be pastors and teachers . . .' (Ephesians 4:11). Is there no significance in the fact that he did not include entertainers in the list?

Yet some people in the pop gospel world even suggest that music is a better medium than words for the communication of the gospel. In a letter from which he has given us permission to quote, Robert Andrews of Chapel Lane Productions says that in certain situations 'when we choose to preach to them using words only, the level of communication is minimal'. Another Christian heavily involved in contemporary Christian music went so far as to say, 'If it is "impossible to communicate the gospel of Romans in music, drama or dance", it is even more impossible for preachers, whose words can go nowhere as far to communicate the depth of the concepts involved.' We wonder what comment that might have produced from Dr Martyn Lloyd-Jones, who managed to keep going through Romans at Westminster Chapel on Friday nights for thirteen years, from 1955-1968, without needing a single note of music to communicate 'the depth of the concepts involved'!

Even more importantly, that philosophy fails to grasp the tremendous truth that preaching cannot be divorced from the gospel. The method and the message are inseparable – and *non-verbal communication does not count as preaching*. To give an obvious example: Paul told the Corinthians, 'For Christ did not send me to baptize, but to preach the gospel' (1 Corinthians 1:17). Baptism is obviously a valid form of communication – one that is biblical and God-ordained – but Paul's point is that it is quite distinct from the preaching of the gospel. Baptism is good, right and biblical, but it is not preaching.

The point becomes even clearer when we take a closer look at Paul's phrase, 'to preach the gospel'. In the original Greek this is just one word – *euangeliseathai,* which we sometimes transliterate 'to evangelize'. But the word Paul uses is a verbal form of the noun *euangelion* – and we would be more strictly accurate to translate his statement: 'Christ did not send me to baptize, but to *gospel.*' The gospel and the preaching of the gospel are as closely linked as that. A little further on in his letter, Paul says that people would have preferred some other form of communication: 'Jews demand miraculous signs and Greeks look for wisdom' (1 Corinthians 1:22). What was Paul's response? God had used him to perform miracles before; why not ask for power to perform more? He certainly had the intellectual capacity to tangle with the Greeks at a rational and philosophical level; why not try to win them over that way? Yet Paul's response was to satisfy neither group. He knew of only one way to meet their need: 'We *preach* Christ crucified' (1 Corinthians 1:23). As far as Paul was concerned, nothing else could properly communicate the gospel, not even the powerful alternatives suggested by some. *If preaching cannot be replaced by miracles, how can it possibly be replaced by music?*

Secondly – and this applies especially to young Christians – you are free to get more closely involved *in the work, worship and fellowship of your local church.* There is no doubt that when young people are heavily involved in the pop gospel scene they tend to drift away from the basic life of the local church. Our experience in countless churches would bear this out almost to the extent that we see a kind of sliding-scale operating. The farther young people are into musical evangelism, the less they tend to support the vital structures of the church, and vice-versa. When music takes over, corporate prayer and Bible study, church involvement and missionary interest (other than the sensational or unusual) decline. A prayer meeting or Bible study probably seems pretty tame after a gospel concert! Even Sunday attendance suffers: we know of young people who will go by the coachload to a gospel concert on a Saturday night, then miss Sunday morning's service. Youth leaders have a particular responsibility here, by example, by encouragement and by the planning of programmes that will help to steer young people in the right direction.

Thirdly, you are free to concentrate on what are clearly *New Testament methods of evangelism.* What are they? Writing in *Evangelical Times,* Geoff Thomas suggested that 'The only New Testament precedents for spreading the gospel are godly living, praying and bold speaking.'[5] That sounds pretty meagre, but it is far from it, because the 'bold speaking' covers an almost endless variety of things. 'Bold speaking' can obviously take place in a pulpit or on a platform, but it can also take place at informal church-based functions or on neutral ground; it can take place at home or at work, at a social or sports club, at school, college or university, in a car, a bus, a train, on board a ship or in an aircraft – in fact wherever two or more people get into conversation. In an Eastern European country recently, church leaders told us that at one stage they had become discouraged at not being able to use many of the evangelistic methods available to us in the West. Then they had second thoughts and decided that they were wrong to feel like that, because they could use all the methods available to the church in the New Testament! As Geoff Thomas adds in his article, 'What turned the world upside down then is sufficient to do it today.'[6] Time saved in advertising, planning, organizing, supporting and attending gospel concerts, religious road shows and the like can be put to better use in activities that have clear New Testament backing.

Fourthly, you are free to spend more time in *personal evangelism*. There is a case for saying that this was the most widely used method of evangelism in the New Testament, and another for saying that it is the most widely neglected in the church today. In his racy paperback *Evangelism – Now and Then*, Michael Green comments, 'This is the biggest difference between the New Testament church and our own. Their responsibility of bearing witness to Jesus rested fairly and squarely upon every single member . . . These days evangelism is spasmodic (if it happens at all), expensive . . . and is dependent upon the skills of the resident evangelist or visiting specialist. This is exceedingly foolish.'[7] One of the reasons it is foolish is that it limits the greatest task in the world to the efforts of a tiny minority of Christians and to a very small fraction of their time. In the business world, that kind of policy would be a recipe for bankruptcy. In a famous report published by the Church of England in 1945 under the title *Towards the Conversion of England*, it was said that 'There will be no widespread evangelization of England unless the work is undertaken by the lay people of the church.'[8] That statement remains true today.

It also helps to pinpoint one of the weaknesses of 'gospel rock' and that is that its 'target area' is so limited. In a nutshell, it is juvenile, appealing almost exclusively to the young. It has little to say to the mature and middle-aged and nothing at all to the elderly, the sick, the dying, or the millions who are turned off by its very style. What is more, there are scores of situations in which it is totally out of place – a house meeting, a funeral, a classroom, a hospital ward, and so on.

On the other hand, verbal communication is relevant to every person, in every place and at any time. There is no situation in which the spoken word may not be an effective vehicle for communicating the gospel, for the simple reason that it is the method God ordained for the purpose.

One of the most exciting things about personal evangelism is that it is something open to every Christian. Have you ever thought of the wisdom of God in this? You do not have to be musical or theatrical, gifted or extrovert, nor do you have to gather an audience or advertise your ability. Going back to Geoff Thomas's three New Testament methods, every Christian can pray, every Christian is called to live a godly life and every Christian can speak about Christ. In his infinite love and wisdom, God has put the greatest privilege in the world within the reach of every Christian believer and as the census we mentioned in chapter six showed, personal evangelism remains one of the most effective means of sharing the gospel.

But realistic and consistent personal evangelism takes time. It means building bridges of personal friendship, investing in people's lives as well as their souls. It means getting to grips with their personal situations, trying to think through their problems, patiently seeking to answer their questions. Personal evangelism is not a hit-and-run affair, nor is it realistically done merely by taking someone along to an evangelistic event of some kind.

Fifthly, you are free to invest more time in *Bible study and prayer*. This is not a change of subject! The key to effective personal witnessing for Christ (and to effective Christian living as a whole) is not to be found in frantic activity, but in the Christian's personal relationship with the Lord. Moving in exciting circles is not the same as getting somewhere! This instruction from the apostle Peter points us in the right direction here: 'But in your hearts set apart Christ as Lord. Always be prepared to give an answer to everyone who asks you to give the reason for the hope that you have' (1 Peter 3:15). But how can a Christian possibly 'be prepared to give an answer' unless he knows what the answer is? Having a copy of the latest translation of the Bible is no substitute for knowing what it says – and our observations would lead us to believe that many young Christians' preoccupation with gospel music (listening, reading, discussing, attending and so on) has been a major factor in reducing the amount of time available to invest in deepening their own spiritual lives by determined Bible study and effective prayer. The loss to the church – and therefore to the kingdom of God – has been incalculable.

The urgent need of the hour is for a generation of Christian young people who are spiritual giants, sold out to God and determined 'to say "No" to ungodliness and worldly passions, and to live self-controlled, upright and godly lives in this present age' (Titus 2:12). Anything that even *tends* to cool that kind of determination marks a point of spiritual tragedy in the life of the person concerned.

Decision time

In writing this book we believe that we have discharged an important responsibility; now the responsibility shifts from author to reader. We have tried to work through the issue thoroughly, carefully and honestly, without at any point being destructively critical of Christians who might not agree with us. We sincerely believe that the case against the use of pop music in evangelism is over-whelming, but we recognize, of course, that our convictions are not binding on others. Our final direction would therefore come straight from Scripture: 'Each one should be fully convinced in his own mind' (Romans 14:5).

The issue with which Paul was dealing at the time (the religious observance of certain days in the Jewish calendar) was not as important as the present one, but his words are powerfully relevant and pinpoint two vital principles. The first two words – 'each one' – emphasize your *liberty*, the birthright of every Christian. You have no reason to be browbeaten by anyone, nor do you have any need to go along with the crowd. The matter under discussion is one between you and God and you have the right and the privilege of exercising your own conscience in the light of the Word of God. Never let the fact that many or even most Christians take a certain line on a particular issue rob you of your own God-given prerogative.

The second principle is that of your *responsibility:* Paul says that a Christian should be 'fully convinced in his own mind'. The phrase 'fully convinced' is one you would use about gathering evidence and also carries with it the sense of being filled to the brim. Bring these two strands of thought together, recognize that this is not just a suggestion but a command, and you have a picture of just how great a responsibility you have. The issue of entertainment evangelism is tremendously important, not least because evangelism is a matter of life and death. It is seeking to rescue those who are 'without hope and without God in the world' (Ephesians 2:12). The question of how the rescue operation should be carried out is not, therefore, something on which vague ideas will do – and to have a 'couldn't care less' attitude

is downright carnal. Here is something about which you
have a responsibility to be 'fully convinced' – up to the
brim! You must weigh up all the evidence and think
carefully and honestly about all the arguments brought
forward. At the same time, you must set aside your own
emotions, tastes, likings and prejudices: in coming to a
biblical conclusion these are irrelevant.

You have a right to your own judgement on the issue,
but as a Christian you have a responsibility to base that
judgement solely on the commands and principles of
Scripture. In other words, what you think must be controlled by what God says.

At the beginning of the year in which he died, the missionary Spencer Walton wrote these words in his diary:
'The will of God – nothing less – nothing more – nothing
else.' On the issue of entertainment evangelism, as on
every other issue, that should be all you want to *know*
and all you want to *do*.

Appendix

The Neurophysiology of Rock
Drs Daniel and Bernadette Skubik

Rhythms for which drums provide or generate the basic beat produce measurable responses in the body's muscular system, brainwave patterns and hormone levels. Briefly, (i) muscle co-ordination and control become synchronized with the basic beat, (ii) brainwave activity itself aligns with the rhythm so generated; and (iii) various hormones (specifically, opiates and sex hormones) are released as a result of electrophysiological synchronization with the rhythm. These results have been regularly documented by various researchers, and though individual subjects may vary in their response over narrow ranges of controlled input, all normal subjects have reacted as indicated when the rhythm exceeds 3-4 beats per second – roughly speaking, a rhythm exceeding the rate of the average heartbeat.

When the beat generates high levels of sensory excitation (that is, when due to the pace of the rhythm and loudness of the music the auditory impact nears maximal reception) the brain is put in a state of stress. This state of stress is measurable in 'driving' brainwave activity. This driving activity occurs in *all* people when highly stimulated; subjective evaluation of the input – such as whether one likes or dislikes the music – is not a factor. To force its activity levels down and to achieve homeostasis, the brain releases the body's natural opioids.

These opioids are naturally produced opiates chemically similar to drugs like morphine. They are used to control the body's sensitivity to pain (raising pain thresholds) and to counteract associated subjectively felt negative emotions (substituting for depression). This response itself can lead to positive arousal and can become addictive. Simply put, one soon *needs* to have opioids released to feel good. An example of this process in action is 'jogger's high' – a state of subjective well-being in the long-distance runner when passing beyond normal pain thresholds, along with an increase in anxiety or depression when running is hindered due to time pressures or injury. Another and more unfortunate link is that spontaneous increases in alcohol consumption are directly related to opioid release: this physiological connection in part underlies the sociological link between rock music and drugs such as alcohol.

There is also considerable evidence that rock music generates or enhances sexual arousal by way of this same process. That is, to high sensory stimulation the body responds with the release of gonadotrophins as well as opioids. The result is a strong connection forged between a stressed fight-or-flight drive state and the young person's developing sexual drive, which then invariably links arousal to aggression. (An example from the animal kingdom to keep in mind here is the beloved magpie: its aggressive behaviour, often irrational in character, is mediated by the dramatic increase in sexual hormones in spring.) Thus, irrespective of the lyrics of the song, rock music communicates aggressive sexuality. It is no accident that secular rock musicians themselves understand these linkages when flaunted in the motto 'Sex-drugs-and rock 'n' roll'.

We tend to think of our primary physical senses (touch, taste, smell, hearing and sight) as separate channels of input each delivering their own message to the brain for processing. Even when we have more than one sense involved at the moment (we hear and see a bird singing in the tree outside our window), we tend to think of the separateness of this sensory input: we could hear the bird without seeing it, and we could see the bird without hearing it. But when we talk about the brain's actual processing of sensory data and how, for example, we can say we know it is *that* bird and not another unseen bird in a different location we hear singing, the picture becomes much more complex. Briefly, because there is a short but sure separation in time between the right and left ears' reception of sound, there is not only the capacity to detect the direction of the sound's source, but also the creation of auditory 'space'. Slower rhythms of music tend to fill this auditory space with an overall sense of continuity and positive holistic compatibility. The fast rhythms of rock music tend to break up this space, regularly producing perceptions of sharp angles and dark colours because of the sharing in auditory and visual space by polysensory neurons. This preservation or breaking of space in turn mediates behaviour: experiments have shown variations in levels of agitation and anxiety linked to types of music – faster music leads to reactionary behaviour (such as lowering the threshold for irritability or impatience) while slower rhythms generally produce calming effects. (In another context, consumers' purchasing habits in shops such as fast food outlets and supermarkets have been shown to correlate significantly with types of music used by the management.)

A few 'information processing stations' in the brain handle a single type of sensory input. Many, though, as noted above, handle several. In experiments using cats, it has been shown that a significant proportion (approximately 30%) of visual neurons of the cat brain process auditory input. Further research using monkeys and human subjects has also demonstrated that specialized areas of the brain process or respond to the processing of auditory and visual input. This is known as sensory convergence or synesthesia, and helps explain the sometimes felt sense of 'seeing sounds' or 'hearing colours'. Because of this convergence, the brain orients or maps sensory input in a reference 'space' for purposes of integrating input and co-ordinating the body's reactions to that input. The areas of the brain involved in this map building are also the areas involved in the integration of both spoken and written language with emotions: thus, the sometimes felt sense of 'good' or 'evil' sounds, and 'comforting' or 'disturbing' visual effects.

The left and right hemispheres of the brain normally operate in tandem when processing sensory data, each contributing to cognitive understanding and regulation of response to environment. Due to the effects on information processing by drum-generated rhythms, cognition and reactions to such stimulus are also affected. Actual changes in states of consciousness have been documented, with associated changes in emotional attachments and moral evaluations. (Thus, what was once undesired becomes attached to the desirable; and often vice versa.) That is, the usual sequential mode of the left hemisphere in processing information becomes 'overloaded', enabling the right hemisphere's capacities to emerge without check. Meaning (whether of words or of one's understanding of the social context) is then related directly to an unmediated emotional felt state. Bypassed are semantic or discursive modes of relating. It has been suggested that long-term use of rock music will affect language skills, memory capacities, and emotional maturity. We today see this documented in studies decrying the decline in college and university students' abilities to absorb discursive materials, manage their social lives, and create meaning attached to future goals.

The conclusion of these studies is two-fold. First, lyrics are of minor importance here. Whether the words are evil, innocuous, or based in Holy Scripture, the over-all neurophysiological effects generated by the music remain the same. There is simply no such thing as Christian rock that is substantively different in its impact. Second, shorter-term implications involve a decrease in receptivity of discursive communication, while long-term implications pose serious questions for rehabilitation of degraded left hemisphere cognitive skills. In less technical jargon and in specific context, *we should expect that abilities to receive or deliver the gospel, to pray discursively, and to study Scripture are compromised.*

References

Chapter 1
1. M. Doney, *Summer in the City*.
2. As above.
3. K. E. Parker, Article 'Music the Cultural Frontier of the Church' in *Windstorm Christian Music*.
4. Quoted in *The Age of Communication*.
5. S. Lawhead, *Rock Reconsidered*.
6. As above.
7. J. Van Zyl, *Reformation Today*.
8. R. Gruver, *Down Beat*.
9. M. Doney, *Summer in the City*.
10. B. Larson, *Rock*.
11. M. Doney, *Summer in the City*.
12. As above.
13. S. Lawhead, *Rock Reconsidered*.
14. M. Doney, *Summer in the City*.
15. N. Cohn, *WopBopaLooBopLopBamBam*.
16. D. Jewell, *The Popular Voice*.
17. M. Doney, *Summer in the City*.
18. D. Jewell, *The Popular Voice*.
19. As above.
20. D. Wilkerson, *Set the Trumpet to thy Mouth*.
21. S. Lawhead, *Rock Reconsidered*.

Chapter 2
1. S. Lawhead, *Rock Reconsidered*.
2. D. Jewell, *The Popular Voice*.

3. W. Shafer, *Rock Music.*
4. A. Salter, *What is Hypnosis?*
5. J. Fuller, *Are the Kids all right?*
6. R. Mesmer, Article 'Hypnotism induced by a Hypnotist' in *Journal of Christian Healing.*
7. B. W. Lex, *Neurobiology of Ritual Dance.*
8. *Life,* 3 October 1969.
9. B. Larson, *The Day Music Died.*
10. I. Stravinsky and R. Craft, *Horizon,* September 1958.
11. B. Larson, *The Day Music Died.*
12. B. Larson, *Rock.*
13. T. McSloy, *National Review,* 30 June 1970.
14. D. M. Lloyd-Jones, *Preaching and Preachers.*
15. D. Winter, *New Singer, New Song.*
16. D. M. Lloyd-Jones, *Preaching and Preachers.*
17. D. Jewell, *The Popular Voice.*
18. M. Doney, *Summer in the City.*
19. *Hit Parader,* February 1982.
20. M. Doney, *Summer in the City.*
21. D. Hanson and R. Fearn, *The Lancet,* 2 August 1975.
22. W. Burns and D. Robinson, *Hearing and Noise in Industry.*
23. *The Lancet,* 2 August 1975.
24. As above.
25. As above.
26. H. Rookmaker, *The Creative Gift.*

Chapter 3

1. *The Sunday Telegraph,* 5 September 1982.
2. As above.
3. S. Frith, *Sound Effects, Youth Leisure and the Politics of Rock.*
4. Daniel and Bernadette Skubik, *The Neurophysiology of Rhythm.*
5. S. Lawhead, *Rock Reconsidered.*
6. *U.S. News and World Report,* 31 October 1977.
7. *Daily Telegraph,* 4 March 1988.
8. *Planet,* October 1981.
9. L. Roxon, *Rock Encyclopaedia.*

10. *Daily Mail,* 23 December 1988.
11. B. Larson, *Rock.*
12. *Rolling Stone,* 22 July 1971.
13. *Rolling Stone,* 25 March 1976.
14. *New Musical Express,* 13 December 1986.
15. *Newsweek,* 21 December 1981.
16. *Rolling Stone,* 19 February 1981.
17. B. Larson, *Rock.*
18. *Circus,* April 1984.
19. B. Larson, *Rock.*
20. *Hit Parader,* February 1982.
21. *Daily Mirror,* 24 November 1981.
22. *Daily Express,* 24 March 1988.
23. *Newsweek,* March 1985.
24. *St. Paul Pioneer Press,* 20 March 1983.
25. T. Palmer, *Born under a Bad Sign.*
26. S. Lawhead, *Rock Reconsidered.*
27. As above.
28. M. Doney, *Summer in the City.*
29. As above.
30. *Rolling Stone,* 7 October 1976.
31. *Rolling Stone,* 9 February 1978.
32. B. Larson, *Rock.*
33. *Billboard,* 11 December 1976.
34. *Daily Express,* 19 December 1983.
35. *U.S.A. Today,* 13 January 1984.
36. *People,* 30 June 1975.
37. *Newsweek,* 4 January 1971.
38. *Rolling Stone,* 17 July 1975.
39. *Rock,* August 1983.
40. *Queen; A Salute.*
41. *Fort Lauderdale News,* 6 March 1969.
42. *Daily Express,* 19 December 1983.
43. *Circus,* 31 January 1976.
44. *Rolling Stone,* 7 January 1971.
45. *Circus,* 23 June 1977.
46. *Daily Express,* 19 December 1983.
47. *Life,* 28 June 1968.
48. *Time,* 3 January 1969.

49. *Newsweek,* 2 April 1979.
50. *Daily Mirror,* 18 November 1981.
51. *Daily Mail,* 21 January 1983.
52. G. Melly, *Revolt Into Style.*
53. As above.
54. *Daily Telegraph,* 23 September 1981.
55. D. A. Noebel, *The Legacy of John Lennon.*
56. S. Lawhead, *Rock Reconsidered.*
57. R. Taylor, *A Return to Christian Culture.*
58. *Buzz,* February 1983.
59. As above.
60. B. Larson, *The Day Music Died.*
61. M. Luther, Preface to *Wittenburg Gesangbuch.*

Chapter 4
1. B. Larson, *Rock and the Church.*
2. L. Morris, *New Bible Dictionary.*
3. Quoted in *New Wine Magazine,* July 1985.
4. *Buzz,* April 1982.
5. As above.
6. *Hit Parader,* November 1968.
7. *Time,* 19 October 1987.
8. B. Larson, *Rock.*
9. *Circus,* December 1981.
10. *Rolling Stone,* 28 October 1971.
11. *Circus,* 26 August 1980.
12. *Rolling Stone,* 12 February 1976.
13. *Hit Parader,* July 1975.
14. As quoted by Rob Mackenzie, *Bands, Boppers and Believers.*
15. *Time,* 15 August 1975.
16. *Circus,* 19 January 1977.
17. *Newsweek,* 10 May 1976.
18. This group is in no way connected with the group 'Genesis' who record on the Pilgrim label.
19. *Rolling Stone,* 26 October 1972.
20. B. Larson, *The Day Music Died.*
21. Rob Mackenzie, *Bands, Boppers and Believers.*
22. *People,* 23 June 1980.

23. *Circus,* 31 July 1983.
24. Quoted in *Buzz,* May 1982.
25. *Circus,* 12 October 1976.
26. *Rolling Stone,* 20 March 1972.
27. *Newsweek,* 27 March 1972.
28. *Time,* 11 September 1978.
29. *Circus,* 22 December 1977.
30. *Rolling Stone,* 1 July 1976.
31. *Circus,* 16 August 1976.
32. *Rolling Stone,* 19 August 1971.
33. *Newsweek,* 4 January 1971.
34. *Buzz,* April 1982.
35. *Circus,* November 1974.
36. *Billboard,* 10 December 1977.
37. *Buzz,* April 1982.
38. T. Palmer, *Born under a Bad Sign.*
39. *People,* 19 July 1976.
40. *Newsweek,* 10 January 1983.
41. *Buzz,* February 1983.
42. S. Leek, *Numerology.*
43. Quoted by T. Sanchez, *Up and Down with the Rolling Stones.*
44. W. B. Key, *Media Sexploitation.*
45. W. B. Key, *The Calm Bake Orgy.*
46. W. B. Key, *Subliminal Seduction.*
47. L. Silverman, Quoted by Art Athens, Article 'Here Come the Mind Manipulators' in *Family Health Magazine,* December 1978.
48. *Newsweek,* 17 May 1982.
49. *New Times Magazine,* 13 May 1977.
50. *Youth Aflame,* October 1982.
51. As above.
52. *The Listener,* as quoted in *Christian Bookseller Review,* November/December 1988.
53. S. Lawhead, *Rock of this Age.*
54. *Time,* 31 October 1969.
55. *Circus,* 22 December 1977.
56. *Rolling Stone,* 12 February 1976.
57. *The Book of Rock Quotes.*

58. B. Larson, *The Day Music Died.*
59. *Time,* 14 March 1983.
60. As above.
61. B. Larson, *Rock and the Church.*
62. *Buzz,* February 1983.
63. *Buzz,* April 1982.
64. B. Larson, *Rock.*

Chapter 5
1. *Esther* Magazine, August 1985.
2. *Time,* 22 September 1967.
3. D. Pichaske, *A Generation in Motion.*
4. *Toronto Daily Star,* 20 June 1970.
5. *Time,* 26 September 1969, as quoted by D. A. Noebel, *The Legacy of John Lennon.*
6. *Circus,* 17 April 1979.
7. As above.
8. *Reader's Digest,* December 1969.
9. *Young Life,* Vol. 56, No. 2.
10. M. Doney, *Summer in the City.*
11. *Circus,* 13 May 1976.
12. *Melody Maker,* 22 October 1988.
13. *Super Rock,* June 1978.
14. *The Listener,* as quoted in *Christian Bookseller Review,* November/December 1988.
15. *Newsweek,* 14 November 1983.
16. *USA Today,* 16 January 1984.
17. *The Book of Rock Quotes.*
18. G. Melly, *Revolt Into Style.*
19. *The Listener,* 11 February 1982.
20. *Saturday Evening Post,* 15 August 1964.
21. J. Lennon, *A Spaniard in the Works.*
22. *Hit Parader,* 19 June 1975.
23. Quoted in *Dallas Morning News,* 29 October 1978.
24. *Time,* 9 November 1970.
25. *Newsweek,* 9 July 1973.
26. B. Larson, *Rock and the Church.*
27. Appendix to J. & M. Prince, *Time to Listen, Time to Talk.*
28. *Leicester Mercury,* 4 January 1982.

29. D. Beaumont, *New Life* (Australia).
30. *Leicester Mercury,* 4 January 1982.
31. B. Larson, *Rock.*
32. *Buzz,* April 1982.
33. As above.
34. D. Porter, *Media.*
35. Quoted in J. & M. Prince, *Time to Listen, Time to Talk.*
36. *Reader's Digest,* February 1970.
37. As above.
38. *Times on Sunday,* 7 June 1987.
39. Quoted in *Contemporary Christian Music,* August-September 1981.
40. As above.
41. C. Scott, *Music: Its secret influence through the ages.*
42. *Daily Mirror,* 2 January 1982.
43. *Reading Chronicle,* 5 November 1982.
44. *Circus,* 13 May 1976.
45. W. Shafer, *Rock Music.*
46. S. Ostrander and L. Schroeder, *Super Learning.*
47. As above.
48. I. K. Taimni, *The Science of Yoga.*
49. W. B. Key, *Subliminal Seduction.*
50. T. Leary, *Politics of Ecstasy.*
51. *Hit Parader Yearbook,* No. 6, 1967.
52. *Star Weekly Magazine,* 26 August 1967.
53. *Hit Parader,* January 1968.
54. *Melody Maker,* 7 October 1967.
55. *The Guardian,* 28 December 1982.

Chapter 6

1. Quoted by C. Barnes, *God's Army.*
2. *Evangelism Today,* December 1981.
3. *The Listener,* as quoted in *Christian Bookseller Review,* November/December 1988.
4. As above.
5. T. Morton, *Christian Graduate,* March 1981.
6. T. Morton, *Solid Rock?*
7. J. Allen, *Solid Rock?*
8. A. W. Tozer, *Man: the Dwelling Place of God.*

9. P. Bassett, *God's Way.*
10. *Evangelical Times,* November 1987.
11. D. Hesselgrave, *Communicating Christ Cross-Culturally.*
12. G. Cray, Appendix to J. & M. Prince, *Time to Listen, Time to Talk.*
13. L. Norman, *Solid Rock?*
14. *Strait,* October 1983.
15. L. Norman, *Solid Rock?*
16. J. Fischer, *Solid Rock?*
17. *Chambers' Twentieth Century Dictionary.*
18. As above.
19. Plato, *Fourth Book of the Republic.*
20. Plato, *The Republic.*
21. Boethius, *De Institutione Musica.*
22. J. Calvin, *Works,* Vol. VI.
23. S. Ostrander and L. Schroeder, *Super Learning.*
24. C. Scott, *Music: Its secret influence through the ages.*
25. G. Stevenson, *Music and your Emotions.*
26. H. Hanson, *American Journal of Psychiatry.*
27. *Daily Mail,* 13 September 1984.
28. B. Larson, *The Day Music Died.*
29. F. Garlock, *The Big Beat.*
30. *The Guardian,* 28 December 1982.
31. As above.
32. M. Schoen, *The Psychology of Music.*
33. C. Girard, *Solid Rock?*
34. Quoted in *Solid Rock?*
35. V. Wright, *Evangelism Today,* December 1981.
36. W. Shafer, *Rock Music.*
37. F. Garlock, *The Big Beat.*
38. J. Fischer, *Solid Rock?*
39. As above.
40. R. Taylor, *A Return to Christian Culture.*
41. F. Schaeffer, *Addicted to Mediocrity.*
42. E. Wright, *Tell the World.*
43. J. Packer, *What is Evangelism? Perspectives of Church Growth.*

Chapter 7
1. Quoted in *Banner of Truth,* January 1977.
2. As above.
3. Quoted by R. Bainton, *Here I Stand.*
4. *Banner of Truth,* January 1977.
5. E. Routley, *Church Music and the Christian Faith.*
6. D. Kidner, *Christian Graduate,* March 1981.
7. A. Barnes, *Barnes' Notes on the New Testament.*

Chapter 8
1. *Buzz,* September 1981.
2. *Buzz,* December 1981.
3. As above.
4. *Buzz.*
5. *Strait,* No. 2.
6. *21st Century Christian,* July 1987.
7. B. Larson, *Rock and the Church.*
8. *21st Century Christian,* December 1987.
9. Quoted by R. Peck, *Rock: Making Musical Choices.*
10. Quoted by Dennis Hunt, *Amy Grant: A Phenomenon in Christian Music.*
11. R. Peck, *Rock: Making Musical Choices.*
12. As above.
13. Quoted in *21st Century Christian,* December 1988.
14. *Buzz.*
15. *Melody Maker,* 22 October 1988.
16. As above.
17. As above.
18. K. Green, *Can God use Rock Music?*
19. K. Green, *Music or Missions?*
20. A. Redpath, *Blessings out of Buffetings.*
21. Quoted in *Solid Rock?*
22. *Cassell's Twentieth Century Dictionary.*
23. As above.
24. P. Bassett, *God's Way.*
25. Quoted in *D. Martyn Lloyd-Jones: The First Forty Years.*
26. *Buzz,* May 1981.
27. As above.

28. D. Porter, *Media*.
29. K. Green, *Music or Missions?*
30. *Evangelical Times,* May 1988.
31. R. Frost, used by permission.
32. A. Tozer, *The Divine Conquest*.
33. A. Tozer, *Of God and Men*.
34. *Evangelical Times,* May 1979.
35. J. Sidlow Baxter, *Rethinking our Priorities*.
36. E. Routley, *Church Music and the Christian Faith*.
37. S. Henderson, *Whose Idea of Fun is a Nightmare?*
38. Quoted in *Time*, 25 April 1969.
39. *Tampa Tribune,* 4 September 1981.
40. *Melody Maker,* 10 February 1968.
41. Quoted by B. Larson, *Rock and the Church*.
42. G. Lees, *High Fidelity,* February 1970.
43. I. Gitler, *Bell Telephone Magazine,* January-February 1970.
44. *Evangelical Times,* April 1975.
45. As above.
46. *Buzz,* May 1981.

Chapter 9
1. *Christian Herald,* 9 January 1988.
2. J. Calvin, *Institutes,* Vol. 2.
3. Augustine, *Confessions*.
4. *Background to the Task*.
5. *Matthew Henry's Commentary*.
6. J. Godwin, *The Devil's Disciples*.
7. D. Wilkerson, *Get your hands off my throat*.
8. K. Green, *Music or Missions?*
9. R. Connolly, *Anatomy of Pop*.
10. *Reformation Today,* November-December 1982.
11. As above.
12. W. Freel, *Survival*.

Chapter 10
1. B. Edwards, *Nothing but the Truth*.
2. As above.
3. G. Wilson, *Romans*.

4. P. Bassett, *God's Way*.
5. *Evangelical Times*, May 1979.
6. As above.
7. M. Green, *Evangelism – Now and Then*.
8. *Towards the Conversion of England*.